Solve It With Salt and Vinegar

Christine Halvorson

Christine Halvorson is the co-author of *Clean & Simple: A Back-to-Basics Approach to Cleaning Your Home* and the author of *The Home Hints Calendar 2000* and *100s of Helpful Hints*. She is a frequent contributor to *The Old Farmer's Almanac* publications, including *Home Owner's Companion*, *Gardener's Companion*, and *Good Cook's Companion*, and works as a freelance writer from her home in Hancock, New Hampshire.

Acknowledgments:

Recipes on pages 145–147, 165–168, and 171–172 are used with permission from the University of Minnesota Extension Service, www.extension.umn.edu.

Recipes on pages 161, 162–163, and 164 are used with permission from Henry Holt and Company, LLC, from *The Thirteen Colonies Cookbook* by Mary Donovan, Amy Hatrak, Frances Mills, and Elizabeth Shull, © 1975 by Praeger Publishers, Inc.

Louis Weber, CEO
Publications International, Ltd.
7373 North Cicero Avenue
Lincolnwood, Illinois 60712

Manufactured in USA.

8 7 6 5 4 3 2

ISBN: 0-7853-6057-3

The Power of Salt and Vinegar

From cleaning house to preserving food to healing aches and pains, salt and vinegar can tackle even the toughest job. Once you start testing out the solutions in this book, you, too, will be amazed by the power of salt and vinegar!

Vinegar's Vigor

In its various forms, vinegar can be a healer, a disinfectant, a preservative, an acid, and a condiment. This list is pretty impressive considering vinegar is a byproduct of something gone bad.

All vinegar starts as alcohol, which is created through the conversion of carbohydrates to sugar. When alcohol ferments, it becomes acetic acid or vinegar. For example, a bunch of grapes deteriorates to become wine, then wine ferments into wine vinegar.

Vinegar has had its share of curative claims over the years. It was once thought to ward off the Black Plague and prevent scurvy. While these ancient "cures" are dubious, more modern claims are not. Recent medical studies have shown that vinegar can draw venom from a jellyfish sting and be used to detect cervical cancer.

Salt's Strength

While there are dozens of ways to use salt at home, the most common use is in making chemical compounds. Salt is key to the manufacture of steel, aluminum, rubber tires, soap, ceramics, textiles, and inks and dyes, not to mention

Types of Vinegar

Balsamic: **Almost all balsamic vinegar is produced in Italy in "grades" that indicate quality.**

Malt: **With a more earthy flavor than wine vinegar, malt vinegar is often sprinkled on fish.**

Rice: **Often used in Asian dishes, rice vinegar has a lighter taste than wine or malt vinegar.**

Wine: **Made from fermented wine, it is chiefly used for salad dressings and marinades.**

thousands more medical applications. Once, mining or extracting salt was so complicated that salt was very expensive and people were often paid their wages in salt.

All animals, including human beings, require sodium for life and health, yet the human body cannot manufacture sodium on its own. When we lack salt, our muscles won't work properly, our food won't digest, our blood circulation is affected, and our heart may stop beating.

Solution After Solution

The following pages will offer hundreds of salt and vinegar solutions for cleaning, cooking, preserving, and more. Before you know it, you'll become a salt and vinegar expert. Following are a few things you should know before you continue.

Whenever we mention "vinegar," we mean distilled white vinegar. In tips or recipes calling for other types of vinegar, we note the specific type. Similarly, the word "salt" means regular table salt, unless otherwise noted.

When a tip or recipe asks you to make a paste, mix a dry ingredient with a liquid ingredient to the consistency of toothpaste. Exact measurements are unimportant.

We've listed some questionable claims in our "Grain of Salt Department." Also look for "Vinegar Vignettes" and "Salt Snippets" for fun facts about vinegar and salt.

Varieties of Salt

Canning and pickling: **These salts contain no additives and are good for cooking, baking, canning, and pickling.**

Kosher: **Used in cooking, this salt has no additives and is more coarse than table salt. It has also been prepared using methods approved for kosher cooking.**

Rock: **Used to deice sidewalks and make ice cream, rock salt is less refined than table salt, has a different color, and comes in large crystals.**

Sea: **This comes from evaporated sea water rather than from mines. It can be used in cooking and appears in beauty treatments and home remedies.**

Seasoned: **This salt is regular table salt that has been mixed with other flavorings from herbs or spices.**

Sour: **Extracted from citrus fruits, sour salt has an interesting tartness that can spice up some dishes.**

Table: **Used for cooking, baking, and seasoning food, table salt is fine-grained and usually contains iodine and an anticaking agent so it will not clump in the box.**

Chapter 1

Kitchen Cleanup

Most people find that the kitchen is the most difficult room in their home to keep clean. And with good reason! With its endless supply of spills, drips, greasy pans, dirty dishes, and foot traffic, kitchen cleanup can certainly feel like an endless series of tasks. But, thanks to salt and vinegar, you don't need a different commercial cleaner to tackle each problem. Indispensable tools in any kitchen, these two ingredients can clean practically anything plus perform some nifty restoration and maintenance tricks.

A+ Solutions for Cleaning Appliances

Coffeemakers and teapots

Remove coffee and mineral stains from the glass pot of an automatic drip coffeemaker by adding 1 cup crushed ice, 1 tablespoon water, and 4 teaspoons salt to carafe when it is at room temperature. Gently swirl mixture, rinse, and then wash as usual.

Buildup in a coffeemaker's brewing system can affect coffee flavor. Get rid of buildup by running 1 brewing cycle of cold water and ¼ cup vinegar. Follow with a cycle of clean water. If you can still smell vinegar, run another cycle using fresh water.

Boil water and ½ cup vinegar in a teakettle for 10 or 15 minutes to help remove any mineral deposits inside the pot and spout. Rinse thoroughly.

Clean a teapot by boiling a 50/50 mixture of vinegar and water for several minutes; let stand for 1 hour. Rinse with water.

Remove tea or coffee stains from light-colored cups and mugs by rubbing stained areas with salt and a little water. Then wash as usual.

Dishwashers

Add ½ cup vinegar to an empty dishwasher, and run rinse cycle. This will open up any clogs in the dishwasher drain lines and deodorize the machine.

Remove hard-water stains from the inside of an automatic dishwasher by loading the dishwasher with glassware and china and then adding ¾ cup household bleach. Run a complete wash cycle, then put 1 cup vinegar in a glass bowl, and place bowl in dishwasher. Run another complete wash cycle.

Microwaves

If your microwave is spattered with old sauces and greasy buildup, place a glass measuring cup with 1 cup water and ¼ cup vinegar inside microwave. Boil for 3 minutes, then remove measuring cup and wipe inside of oven with a damp sponge.

To remove the lingering smell of burned microwave popcorn, heat a small glass dish of pure vinegar in microwave for 5 minutes, then remove and wipe down inside of oven.

Deodorize your microwave by keeping a dish of vinegar inside overnight. If smells continue, change vinegar and repeat procedure nightly.

Ovens

Twice a year you should "de-grease" the vents of your oven hood. To do this, wipe vents with a sponge and undiluted vinegar, or remove vents and soak them for 15 minutes in 1 cup vinegar and 3 cups water.

If a pie or similar sugary item boils over in your oven, sprinkle the sticky spill with salt. Let it sit until spilled area becomes crisp, then lift off with a spatula when oven cools.

When cleaning your oven, finish the job by using a sponge to wipe entire surface with a mixture of half vinegar and half water. This will help prevent grease buildup.

After cleaning your oven with commercial cleaners, an odor often remains. To eliminate odor, mix 2 cups vinegar and 3 quarts warm water. Dip a sponge into mixture and wring it well, then wipe the oven's inside surfaces. No need to rinse.

Combine ½ cup vinegar and ½ cup hot water together in a small bowl. Use this solution and a sponge to rub away any stained areas in your oven.

Salt Snippet

Salt was once a symbol of incorruption, and, therefore, making a covenant of salt was a binding agreement that was thought to last forever. For example, a passage from the Old Testament says, "The Lord God of Israel gave the kingship . . . to David . . . by a covenant of salt" (2 Chronicles 13:5 NRSV).

Refrigerators

To clean and refresh the inside of your refrigerator, sprinkle equal amounts salt and baking soda on a damp sponge, and wipe refrigerator surfaces.

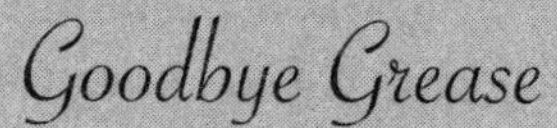

Goodbye Grease

Combine the following ingredients to cut grease buildup on stoves, backsplashes, or glossy enamel surfaces: 3 cups baking soda, 2 cups white vinegar, 1 cup ammonia, and 1 gallon hot water.

Wear rubber gloves, and wipe on mixture, making sure room is well-ventilated.

Prevent mildew buildup inside your refrigerator or on its rubber seals by wiping occasionally with a sponge dampened in undiluted vinegar. No need to rinse afterward.

Remove any mildew spots in or on your refrigerator by scrubbing with an old toothbrush dipped in vinegar. A toothbrush is an excellent tool for reaching inside the folds of the rubber seals.

Stoves

Any spill on your stovetop can be cleaned up more easily if sprinkled with salt first. The mildly abrasive quality of salt removes stuck-on food, but it won't mar the surface.

Clean burned-on food from a stovetop burner by sprinkling it with a mixture of salt and cinnamon, then wipe away immediately. The mixture will give off a pleasant smell and cover up any burnt odor the next time you turn on the burner.

Soak up a liquid spill on a stovetop burner by sprinkling it with a mixture of salt and cinnamon. Leave it on spill for 5 minutes to absorb excess liquid, then wipe away.

Copper as Shiny as a New Penny

Make your copper-bottom pans worthy of display. Sprinkle tarnished bottoms with salt, then scour stains away with a cloth dampened with vinegar. Rinse, then wash as usual. Another tarnish-fighting trick for copper pans: Use a spray bottle to apply undiluted vinegar to bottom of pan. Leave vinegar on pan until you can see tarnish evaporating. Next sprinkle vinegar with salt, and scrub entire surface with scrubbing sponge. Rinse, and repeat if necessary.

Cleaning Cookware Couldn't Be Easier

Casserole dishes

When you're faced with stubborn, baked-on food in a casserole dish, add boiling water and 3 tablespoons salt to dish. Let stand until water cools, then wash as usual.

Egg poachers

To prevent egg poachers or double boilers from becoming discolored, add 1 teaspoon vinegar to the boiling water.

Remove discoloration in an egg poaching pan by heating 1 tablespoon vinegar and 1 quart water in pan until discoloration disappears.

Pots and pans

Get rid of excess grease in a roasting pan by first sprinkling it with salt. Then wipe pan with a damp sponge or paper towel, and wash as usual.

Take care of a really greasy frying pan by simmering ¼ inch water and ½ cup vinegar in it for 10 minutes. The lingering oily smell or residue should disappear. Wash and rinse.

Lingering grease on any type of pan can be cut by filling pan with ¼ inch of water and ½ cup vinegar. Simmer on stovetop for 20 minutes, then wash.

Aluminum pans can develop ugly dark stains over time. Remove stains by boiling pans in a large kettle, using 2 tablespoons vinegar and enough water to cover.

Clean the burned-on mess off a broiler pan by adding 2 cups vinegar and ¼ cup sugar to pan while it is still warm. Soak pan for an hour, then clean as usual.

Simply Sparkling Sinks

Clogs

A mixture of equal parts vinegar, salt, and baking soda may help open up a slow-draining sink. Pour solution down drain, let it sit 1 hour, then pour boiling or very hot tap water down drain.

A sink clog made up of greasy foods may be moved with ½ cup salt and ½ cup baking soda. Sprinkle this solution into drain, then flush with hot tap water.

Clear a minor sink clog with a mixture of ½ cup baking soda and ½ cup vinegar. Let stand 3 hours, then flush with hot water.

Cast Away the Rust

Cast-iron pans, which are often the best choice for cooking some dishes, tend to rust easily if you put them away while slightly damp. Remove rust by soaking pan for several hours in a solution of 2 parts white vinegar to 1 part water. Scrub rusted area with a plastic scrubber, and rinse. If rust remains, repeat.

You'll have to re-season your pan after this rust-removal treatment. To season, wash pan in warm, soapy water, and dry well. Then rub pan with a generous amount of vegetable oil. Heat pan in a 350°F oven for 2 hours, then wipe away any excess oil before use.

Odors

Pour a strong salt solution of 1 cup salt and 2 cups hot water down kitchen drain to eliminate drain odors and break up grease deposits.

Pour ¼ cup each baking soda, salt, and dishwasher detergent into your garbage disposal. Turn on hot water, then run garbage disposal for a few seconds to clean out any debris and clear odors.

The rubber seal on garbage disposals can retain odors. To deodorize it, remove seal and let it soak in a pan of white vinegar for 1 hour.

Stains

Tackle mineral deposits around your sink's faucets by squirting them with undiluted vinegar. Let vinegar sit 15 minutes or more, then scrub away deposits with an old toothbrush.

Clean minor stains in a white porcelain sink with a sprinkling of baking soda and a sponge dampened in vinegar. Stains are best tackled immediately.

For tough or aged stains in a white porcelain sink, cover stained areas with paper towels saturated in household bleach (wear rubber gloves and make sure room is well-ventilated). Leave paper towels for ½ hour or until they dry out. Remove towels, and rinse area thoroughly.

Follow this treatment by cleaning sink with pure vinegar to remove bleach smell.

Multipurpose Home Cleaner

Eliminate the need for several expensive commercial cleaning products from your shelf with the following mixture: 1 teaspoon borax, ½ teaspoon washing soda*, 2 teaspoons vinegar, ¼ teaspoon or 1 squirt liquid dish soap, and 2 cups hot water.

***Washing soda is just a stronger form of baking soda. You can substitute 1 teaspoon baking soda for washing soda.**

Prepare mixture, and store it in a clean, spray bottle. You might want to recycle an old spray bottle from one of the commercial cleaners, or you can buy brand-new empty bottles at most hardware stores. Make sure you clearly label bottle and attach a list of its ingredients.

Use cleaner on virtually any surface in your kitchen for daily cleaning. It is especially good for cleaning stovetops and ovens. For caked-on stains on your stovetop, spray on mixture and let sit 15 minutes before wiping surface clean. To clean the inside of your oven, spray on cleaner, leave overnight, and wipe clean.

Putting the Shine Back on Kitchen Surfaces

Countertops

Wipe your kitchen countertops with straight vinegar once a day to shine them and keep your kitchen smelling fresh.

For everyday cleaning of tile and grout, rub with a little apple cider vinegar on a sponge. This gives off a pleasant scent and will help cut any greasy buildup.

Clean out the Grout!

Tile countertops can be an extremely attractive feature of any kitchen—until the white grout gets grungy and stained with dirt and food. Clean grout with this homemade mixture: 2 cups vinegar, 1 cup clear ammonia, 3 cups baking soda, and 1 gallon warm water.

Protect your hands with rubber gloves, then apply solution with a sponge. Scrub with an old toothbrush if grout is heavily soiled.

Wood

Clean a wood cutting board with soap and a little water. Follow cleaning by wiping board with a damp cloth dipped in salt until salt is gone. The salt treatment will leave the board looking and feeling fresh. (Never cut meat, poultry, or fish on a wood cutting board.)

Wooden bread boxes tend to become sticky with fingerprints and food. You can freshen one easily by wiping surface with vinegar on a sponge or cloth. Do this periodically to prevent grime buildup. A heavy buildup may require repeated wipes with a sponge dampened with vinegar and sprinkled with salt.

Vinegar Vignette

If you pour oil and vinegar into the same vessel, you would call them not friends but opponents.

—Aeschylus

Useful Utensils That Look Great, Too!

Flatware

Clean streaks on your everyday flatware by rubbing them with a soft cloth sprinkled with a little olive oil. Use a second cloth to buff.

Silverware

The tarnish on silverware can be removed by gently rubbing pieces with salt and a soft cloth and then washing them by hand with dish soap and warm water.

To clean sterling silver pieces and bring back their shine, rub them with a paste made of ½ cup vinegar and 2 tablespoons salt. Dip a clean, soft cloth in the paste, then gently rub silver pieces using a circular motion. Rinse, then dry with another soft cloth.

Fill a large bowl with distilled white vinegar, and then add baking powder until mixture starts to bubble. Dip silver pieces into solution for a few seconds, then buff tarnished areas with a clean, soft cloth. If tarnish remains, repeat process, leaving silver pieces in mixture for a longer period of time. Buff again.

Utensils

If mineral deposits have built up on your aluminum kitchen utensils, add a few tablespoons vinegar to a pot of boiling water. Drop utensils in the water, and boil them for about 5 minutes. Rinse with fresh water.

Salt Snippet

Some people consider spilling salt to be unlucky. This superstition dates back to at least the early days of Rome. In the painting "The Last Supper" by Leonardo da Vinci, Judas Iscariot, who betrayed Jesus to the authorities, is shown among the other disciples with a salt cellar knocked over by his arm.

Remove streaks on your stainless-steel kitchen utensils or bowls by rubbing them with a little olive oil. Dampen a cloth with vinegar, and buff each piece to a shine. This treatment will also work for stains on your flatware.

Your Tableware Never Looked So Good!

Dishes

When you can't wash the breakfast dishes immediately, sprinkle plates with salt to prevent any egg from sticking. This will make dishes easier to clean when you do have time.

Kitchen-Fresh Cleaner

Try this homemade recipe for a basic everyday cleaner in your kitchen: 5 drops peppermint oil or any essential oil for fragrance, ¼ cup vinegar, 1 squirt liquid dish soap, and enough water to fill a 32-ounce bottle. It won't tackle the tough, greasy jobs, but using it daily can help control grease buildup, remove spills, and keep your kitchen smelling nice. In fact, you can customize the essential oil fragrance to suit your taste. (The oil is only for fragrance and will not affect the cleaning ability of this solution.)

Keep the kitchen cleaner in a spray bottle, and make sure you clearly label its contents. Shake well before each use. Spray cleaner on countertops and appliances, then wipe off with a damp cloth or sponge.

Glassware

Get rid of the cloudy film on glassware by soaking it overnight in a tub of 1 part vinegar to 1 part warm water. Wash glasses by hand the next day.

Crystal is best washed by hand, very carefully. After washing, dip crystal in a sink full of warm water and 1 tablespoon vinegar. Finish with a clear water rinse from the sink's spray handle.

Eliminate odors from glass jars by filling them with warm water and 2 tablespoons vinegar. Shake well and let stand 2 hours. Wash as usual.

Odor Eaters

Plastic

Freshen a plastic lunch box by filling it with water and ¼ cup vinegar. Let stand for 12 hours.

Sprinkle some salt into a thermos or any closed container prone to developing odors. Leave overnight, then rinse. Smells should disappear, but repeat if necessary.

Vinegar Vignette

To make a good salad is to be a brilliant diplomatist—the problem is entirely the same in both cases. To know exactly how much oil one must put with one's vinegar.

—Oscar Wilde

Sponges

Refresh a fading sponge by washing it in your dishwasher. Use a clothespin to clip it to top rack of dishwasher. After cleaning, soak sponge in cold saltwater to revive its fibers.

Soak a well-worn, smelly sponge in a shallow dish of vinegar for several hours. Rinse sponge well, then let dry.

During very humid weather, store your kitchen sponge in a shallow bowl of vinegar to keep it from souring.

Wood

You can remove odors from wood or plastic cutting boards by sprinkling a damp sponge with baking soda and wiping board. Follow this by wiping board with a sponge dampened with a little vinegar.

Get the Lead Out

Most people know that ingesting lead or lead-base products can cause health problems. The foil wrapper on wine bottles is designed to keep air out of the wine and protect the cork from pests. However, it can actually contain lead that is harmful to swallow. To remove lead residue before pouring wine, remove entire wrapper from bottle and discard. Then wipe rim and neck of bottle with a cloth dampened in vinegar. The acid in vinegar neutralizes any traces of lead.

Stale smells in any type of bread box can be eliminated by placing a small bowl of vinegar inside overnight.

More Tips and Tricks Around the Kitchen

Baby bottle nipples

Add 1 tablespoon vinegar to 8 ounces water in a wide-mouth glass measuring cup. Add baby bottle nipples, and boil in microwave for 2 minutes.

Fires

Extinguish a small grease fire with loose salt. This method works for a burner fire or a fire inside the oven. (Use caution when putting out fires, and do not hesitate to use a fire extinguisher or call for help if a fire intensifies.)

Silence your smoke detector during a cooking disaster by dampening a dishtowel with vinegar and waving it in the smoky area.

> Salt Snippet
>
> **Ice cream makes its debut in Italy in 1559, as it's discovered that ice and salt make a freezing combination.**

Boil 1 tablespoon vinegar in 1 cup water to eliminate smoky smells.

Fruit flies

Set a small saucer of ¼ cup vinegar and 1 drop liquid soap near areas where fruit flies are gathering. The vinegar will attract flies and keep them off your fruit.

Spills

Picking up the mess from a dropped egg can be tricky. Make it easier by sprinkling it with salt; let stand 15 minutes. The salt absorbs and solidifies the runny egg. Wipe away with a paper towel.

If you spill a small amount of vegetable or cooking oil on the floor, sprinkle it with salt, and let sit. Wipe up spill after about 15 minutes.

Vegetables

Keep a spray bottle of vinegar near your kitchen sink, and use it to spritz vegetables before you rinse them with cold running water. The vinegar will help dissolve pesticide residue.

Vinegar Vignette

In 1756, the duc de Richelieu invented the recipe for mayonnaise with his particular mixture of egg yolks, vinegar, oil, and seasonings. The name may have come from a town in Minorca, an island off of Spain.

Washing dishes

Put a few tablespoons vinegar in the sink when washing dishes. The vinegar will cut grease, make dishes shine, and help your soap work harder.

Give your dish soap a powerful boost by adding 5 tablespoons vinegar to a nearly full bottle. Shake well to mix before each use.

Chapter 2

Cleaning House

Are you ready to be astounded by vinegar's power over that grunge in your bathroom and awed by salt's ability to clean a carpet? Well, that's just the beginning! Salt and vinegar are extraordinary cleaning and deodorizing agents for your entire home. This chapter includes various recipes for homemade cleaning solutions that can hold their own against many of today's commercial products. So stock your cupboard with salt and vinegar, and get ready to tackle your home's toughest cleaning jobs.

Make Your Bathroom Brighter

Bathtubs

A bathtub ring requires a strong solvent. Try soaking paper towels with undiluted vinegar and placing them on ring. Let towels dry out, then spray with straight vinegar and scrub with a sponge.

Once a year, dump 1 gallon vinegar into your hot tub, and run it. This will help keep jets from clogging up with soap residue.

Decal Duty

Those sunflower decals may have looked cute when you stuck them on the tub to prevent slips and falls, but now they're chipped, stained, and probably out of fashion. To get rid of them, loosen the glue by saturating each decal with vinegar. (Warm vinegar in microwave for about 3 minutes for even better results.) Let vinegar sit for a few minutes, then peel off decals. You should be able to remove any leftover glue with a damp sponge.

Showers

Showerheads can get clogged with mineral deposits from your water. Remove deposits by mixing ½ cup vinegar and 1 quart water in a large bowl or bucket. Remove showerhead and soak it in vinegar solution for 15 minutes. For plastic showerheads, soak for 1 hour in a mixture of 1 pint vinegar and 1 pint hot water.

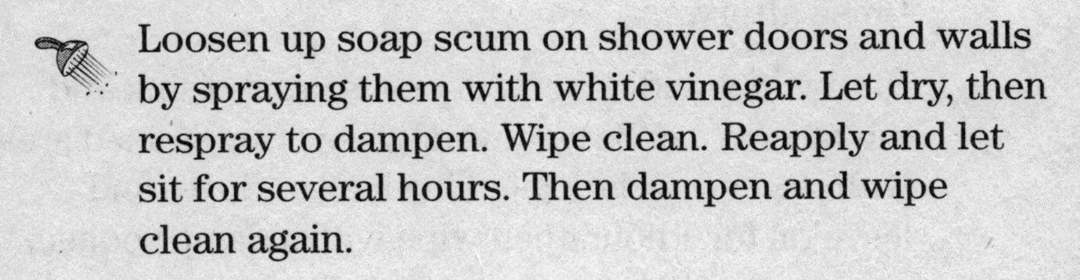

Loosen up soap scum on shower doors and walls by spraying them with white vinegar. Let dry, then respray to dampen. Wipe clean. Reapply and let sit for several hours. Then dampen and wipe clean again.

Fiberglass shower and tub surrounds need special care because fiberglass scratches easily. Clean these areas periodically by spraying them with vinegar and wiping with a sponge. Never use abrasive cleaners—instead, try baking soda and a sponge dampened with vinegar.

Shower curtains can become dulled by soap film or plagued with mildew. Keep vinegar in a spray bottle near shower, and squirt shower curtains once or twice a week. No need to rinse.

Sometimes mildew will leave a stain on shower curtains if not promptly removed. To remove such stains, mix borax with enough vinegar to make a paste, then scrub stained area.

Sinks

Make a paste of turpentine mixed with salt to restore white enameled fixtures that have gone yellow. Use this on sinks, bathtubs, or toilets. Apply, let sit 15 minutes, then wipe with a damp sponge.

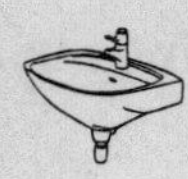
Discolored white enamel can be cleaned with a cloth saturated with turpentine and dipped in salt. Rinse afterward.

Hard-water and mineral deposits around sink and tub faucets can be removed by covering stained area with paper towels soaked in vinegar. Cover and leave on for 1 hour, then wipe with a damp sponge.

Plug drain in bathroom sink, pour in ½ cup white vinegar, then fill sink with water. Let sit 1 hour, then scrub any mineral deposit areas with an old toothbrush. Rinse.

Mix equal amounts of white vinegar and water in a spray bottle. Spray onto moldy or mildewed areas and let sit for 15 minutes. Wipe clean. Use solution occasionally as a preventative measure in any area of your home that is prone to being damp, such as under a sink or in the cellar.

Toilets

Pour vinegar into toilet and let sit 30 minutes. Next sprinkle baking soda on a toilet bowl brush and scour any remaining stained areas. Flush.

Once a week, pour 2 cups vinegar into toilet and let it sit. (Tip: Rest toilet bowl brush inside bowl with lid closed to remind yourself and family members not to use the toilet until it gets brushed!) After 8 hours or more, brush toilet well, and flush. This regular treatment will keep hard-

water stains at bay and clean and freshen your bowl between major cleanings.

Magic Carpet Cleaners

The first rule of carpet cleaning is to wipe up any spill or stain immediately. Often undiluted vinegar can be your best bet for removing a new stain.

Multipurpose Cleaning Solution

This is a great general cleaner to always keep on hand for standard cleaning projects around the home. Just mix 1 teaspoon liquid soap or borax, a splash of white vinegar, and 1 quart warm water. Keep solution in a clean spray bottle, and clearly label contents. Shake well before each use.

For general cleanup of problem areas on carpets or rugs, use equal parts distilled vinegar and water. Lightly sponge solution into carpet, rinse, and blot dry. Let dry before using area again.

Catsup

Remove catsup from a rug by sponging a mixture of 1 cup vinegar and 2 cups water into rug. Frequently wring out sponge until stain is gone.

Chewing gum

To dissolve chewing gum stuck in carpet or any cloth, saturate area with vinegar and let sit briefly.

(For faster results, heat vinegar first.) Carefully tug at gum to remove it.

Chocolate

Chocolate stains can be cleaned with 1 part vinegar and 2 parts water. Sponge on mixture, and blot stain with lots of clean cloths until gone.

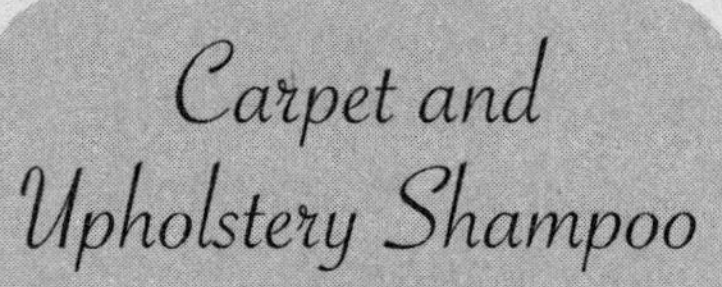

Use an eggbeater to combine 1 quart water, ¼ cup mild powdered detergent, and 1 tablespoon white vinegar. Whip until a stiff foam forms. Gently rub solution into fabric or carpeting, then remove soiled foam with a dull knife. Follow with a rinse of clean water.

Coffee

Coffee spilled on a rug should come out easily with plain water if you attack it immediately. If not, mix 1 part vinegar to 2 parts water, and sponge solution into rug. Blot up any excess, and rinse until brown color is gone.

Cola

Immediately blot a cola spill with paper towels, then clean area with 1 part vinegar to 2 parts water.

Crayon

Remove crayon stains from carpeting or any other fabric or surface by scrubbing area with a toothbrush dipped in vinegar.

Glue

A well-dried spot of white school glue can be taken out of a carpet with 1 part vinegar to 2 parts water. Just sponge on mixture and blot. If spot is stubborn, cover it with warm vinegar and let sit for 10 to 15 minutes. When glue has softened, either scrape it up using a dull knife or blot with paper towels.

Gravy

For a gravy stain on carpet, first remove as much liquid as possible by covering spot with salt. This will prevent the greasy stain from spreading. Then follow rug manufacturer's instructions. You may need a dry-cleaning solution or an enzyme detergent.

Grease

Try removing grease spots in a rug with a mixture of 1 part salt to 4 parts rubbing alcohol. Rub hard, going the same direction as the nap, then rinse with water.

Ink

An ink stain on a carpet or rug should be treated immediately by blotting and spraying stained area with hair spray. Once ink spot is gone, work a solution of half vinegar, half water into area to remove sticky spray.

Mildew

Once mildew gets into a rug, it lives and grows. Kill it with a 50/50 mixture of vinegar and water. Make sure rug dries completely. You may want to use a hair dryer set on low to speed up drying time.

Red wine

Immediately blot up all moisture from spill, then sprinkle area with salt. Let sit 15 minutes. The salt should absorb any remaining wine in the carpet (turning pink as a result). Then clean entire area with a mixture of ⅓ cup vinegar and ⅔ cup water.

Spot's Stains

To clean up messes made by your pet, first scrape up solids and blot liquids, then clean rug with a rug cleaner. After cleaning, rinse with a mixture of ¼ cup vinegar to 1 cup water to remove all trace of smell and to discourage a repeat performance. Pets are attracted to areas that smell like them, so this is a vital step in your carpet cleaning.

Salt residue

Mix equal amounts of vinegar and water, and apply solution with a sponge to salt deposits on your rug or carpet. Do not saturate. Let dry, then vacuum.

Urine

Urine accidents of any sort should be rinsed immediately with warm water. Then mix 3 tablespoons white vinegar and 1 teaspoon liquid soap. Apply solution to stained area and leave on 15 minutes. Rinse, and rub dry.

Care for Bare Floors

Ceramic tile

One cup vinegar and 1 gallon warm water mopped onto ceramic tile floors will make them sparkle.

Linoleum and vinyl

Scrub a linoleum floor with a mixture of 1 gallon water and 1 cup vinegar. If floor needs a polish after this, use straight club soda.

If you've performed a wax-stripping operation on your kitchen floor using ammonia, finish the project by rinsing entire floor with a solution of 1 gallon water and

Carpet Rinse

This treatment will help keep your carpet fresh and clean longer between shampoos. Combine ¼ cup vinegar and 1 gallon water, then use solution in a steam-cleaning vacuum after shampooing your carpet to remove any shampoo residue.

½ cup vinegar. The vinegar will remove lingering wax and the ammonia smell.

If you use detergent on your no-wax vinyl or linoleum floor, rinse afterward with a solution of 1 cup vinegar to 1 gallon water.

Mop up salt deposits from winter boots with a mixture of half vinegar, half water.

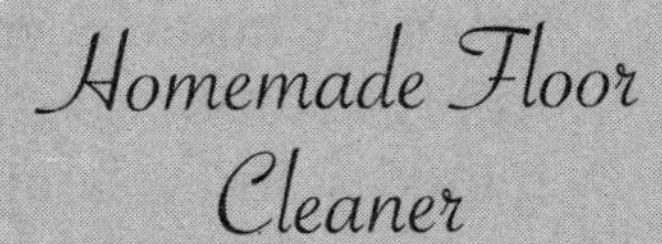

Here's a simple, homemade solution for cleaning laminate and tile floors. Combine 1 part white vinegar, 1 part rubbing alcohol, 1 part water, and 3 drops dishwashing liquid. This mixture can be used to clean the entire floor, or keep it in a spray bottle and use for spot cleaning and deodorizing.

Terra-cotta tile

Wash grout between terra-cotta tiles with straight vinegar to clean up and prevent smudges.

Wood

Add a cup of plain vinegar to a gallon bucket of water, and mop lightly onto hardwood floors (do not saturate). No need to rinse. This will keep floors shiny and remove any greasy buildup.

A closet with bare wood floors can become stale smelling. To freshen them, lightly mop with a mixture of 1 cup baking soda and ½ cup vinegar in 1 gallon warm water.

Revitalize Your Furniture

Leather

A leather desktop can develop a waxy buildup from polish. Remove buildup with a solution of 1 tablespoon vinegar in 1 cup warm water. Wipe on with a soft cloth, then buff dry.

Pianos

Whiten the ivory keys of a piano by rubbing with a little white vinegar on a soft white cloth. Do not saturate.

Vinyl

Spots on vinyl furniture can be removed by wiping with a cloth dipped in straight vinegar.

Wicker

Keep white wicker furniture from yellowing by scrubbing it with a stiff brush moistened with saltwater. Scrub, then let piece dry in full sunlight.

Wood

When a hot dish or water has marred the surface of a wood table, get rid of the mark with a thin paste made of salad oil and salt. Just wipe on paste, then buff slightly as you wipe off with a soft cloth.

Labels, decals, tape, or any sticky paper product can be removed from wood furniture by dampening with straight vinegar. Let sit for a few minutes, then peel or gently scrape off.

Waxy buildup of grease and cleaners on wood tabletops can be removed by applying a solution of equal parts water and vinegar. Wipe onto area, then rub and dry immediately using a soft cloth.

To restore luster to mahogany furniture, mix 3 tablespoons white vinegar and 1 quart water. Dip a sponge in mixture, wring thoroughly, then use to wipe wood. Do not saturate.

Working With Metal

Brass and copper

To clean and shine copper or brass surfaces, make a paste out of equal parts salt, flour, and vinegar. Rub on with a soft cloth, let sit about 1 hour, then wipe off and buff with a clean, soft cloth.

Basic Furniture Polish

Make your own polish for general use on all wood furniture. Whisk ½ teaspoon light olive oil and ¼ cup white vinegar in a small bowl. Pour mixture into a clean, resealable jar, and label clearly. When ready to use, give jar a good shake, then apply polish liberally to wood surfaces with a soft cloth. Wipe away all excess.

Clean tarnish off copper decorative pieces by spraying them with vinegar and sprinkling with salt. Scrub pieces with a sponge, then rinse carefully, making sure to remove all salt traces. Repeat if necessary.

A paste of equal parts salt and flour and enough vinegar to congeal can also be used to clean and polish copper. Apply solution to item with a soft cloth, then rinse and dry with another cloth.

Linseed Furniture Polish

Make this polish just before using; otherwise, it will become too sticky.

Mix 1 tablespoon boiled linseed oil, 1 tablespoon white vinegar, and 1 tablespoon turpentine in a jar with a sealed lid. Shake well before using. Dampen a soft cloth with cold water, wringing it out as much as possible. Then saturate cloth with mixture, and apply to a small area. Let it dry on the furniture for about a half hour, then wipe and polish area.

Clean slightly tarnished brass or copper with a sliced lemon dipped in salt.

Chrome

Chrome fixtures, such as oven handles or mirror frames, can be cleaned of spots by simply wiping with plain vinegar. If heavily soiled, wipe chrome with a sponge dampened with vinegar and sprinkled with a little baking soda.

Window Washing Made Easier

The simplest and easiest method of making window cleaner is to add 2 tablespoons vinegar to 1 cup water. Spray solution on windows, and wipe with paper towels.

Many people use newspapers and vinegar to wash their windows. Just pour vinegar into a shallow container, crumple newspaper, and dip. Wipe window clean, then use a dry newspaper for a final wipe.

Another window-cleaning solution is to fill a clean,

Pewter Cleaner

Pewter must be cleaned gently because it is a soft metal that can be damaged easily. Follow this recipe to make a safe yet mildly abrasive paste.

Add flour to a mixture of 1 teaspoon salt and 1 cup vinegar until you can make a smooth paste. Apply paste to pewter piece. Allow to dry for a half hour, then rinse with warm water. Polish with a soft cloth, being careful to remove paste residue from all grooves or hidden areas.

empty spray bottle with ½ cup vinegar, ¼ cup rubbing alcohol, and enough water to fill. Spray on windows or glass, and wipe with paper towels.

Clean your car windows, whether plastic or glass, with a solution of ¼ cup vinegar in 1 gallon warm water. Rinse, and dry with a clean cloth.

Combine 1 quart warm water, ¼ cup white vinegar, and 2 tablespoons olive oil. Dampen a soft cloth with cleaner, and wipe on wood paneling. Dry area with another clean, soft cloth.

More Home Cleaning Tips and Tricks

Baby toys

Disinfect baby toys by cleaning them with a splash of vinegar added to hot water or by soaking them in a dishpan of hot water and ½ cup white vinegar.

Computers

Clean smudges off your computer monitor frame with a cotton ball dampened with vinegar (do not touch the cotton ball to the computer screen). This also works for keyboard smudges. Be careful not to saturate.

Wall Cleaner

Make this special solution to celebrate spring cleaning in your home. Take the time to do all the walls in your home, whether they look dirty or not. They probably are, and regular cleaning will extend the life of your paint. You can also use this mixture to clean the wood window and door frames in your home.

Mix together 1 gallon water, 1 cup ammonia, ½ cup vinegar, and ¼ cup baking soda in a large bucket. Stir thoroughly. Wash walls with solution from top to bottom, using a clean sponge and rinsing often. Stir mixture occasionally during use. Ventilate each room as you work to avoid breathing ammonia fumes.

Fireplace bricks

Soiled fireplace bricks can be cleaned with a stiff bristled brush dipped in white vinegar.

Humidifier

If you use a humidifier in your home, remove the filter occasionally and soak it in white vinegar. The buildup of sediment should come off easily. Then wash filter with dish soap.

Odors

Mix 1 teaspoon baking soda, 1 tablespoon vinegar, and 2 cups water. Mix well (until foaming stops), then store in a spray bottle. Spray it anywhere you want to eliminate or control household odors.

Pour vinegar into shallow bowls, and set in areas of your home where odors are a problem. The vinegar absorbs odors and can work particularly well to eliminate the smell of burned food or cooked fish in your kitchen.

Place a small bowl of white vinegar in a room where people have been smoking to absorb odor.

Set out bowls of vinegar in a room that has been newly painted. The vinegar will keep the new paint smell under control. Change vinegar once a day and continue for about 3 days.

Homemade Cleaning Spray

Here's another recipe for a homemade cleaner to replace commercial cleaners. This one is great for cleaning dirty fingerprints off walls and door frames.

In a clean spray bottle, mix together 1 teaspoon baking soda, 1 teaspoon borax, 2 teaspoons lemon juice or white vinegar, 3 teaspoons liquid dish soap, and 2 cups hot water. (Make sure you clearly label bottle to alert other household members.) Shake well before each use. Spray on trouble areas about once a week.

Telephone

Clean your telephone with a cotton swab dipped in undiluted vinegar. This is great for removing fingerprints and smudges from the plastic parts of white or light-colored telephones. Be careful not to saturate.

Vases

Remove mineral deposits or stains from a flower vase by dampening with water then adding salt. Wipe with a cloth.

For out-of-reach deposits in narrow flower vases, add a strong salt and water solution to vase, shake, and swirl. Let stand 15 minutes, then rinse and wash with soap and water.

Wallpaper

Mix ½ cup vinegar and 1 quart water, and apply solution to dirty wallpaper using a sponge. Be careful not to saturate, especially at seams and corners, or you could loosen wallpaper.

Grime Cleaner for Radiators

Clean radiators, heating vents, and heat returns with the following mixture: ½ cup vinegar, 1 cup ammonia, ¼ cup baking soda, and 1 gallon hot water.

Use this solution only in a well-ventilated area to dilute ammonia fumes. Wear rubber gloves to protect your hands, then apply cleaner with a sponge or cloth. This solution also works well on soiled walls.

Chapter 3

Home Improvement

The chemical properties of salt and vinegar make them useful for many common repair and maintenance jobs around the house. You can use salt to make your own plaster, while vinegar keeps painting odors at bay and can remove sticky things like furniture glue, wallpaper paste, and adhesive decals from a variety of surfaces. Both ingredients do wonders at removing rust and cleaning surfaces to prepare for painting or staining. The list of solutions is endless!

Adventures in Painting and Staining

Metal

Before painting a metal item, wipe surface with a solution of 1 part vinegar to 5 parts water. This cleans the surface and makes peeling less likely.

Galvanized metal should be scoured with vinegar before painting. The acidic qualities of vinegar will clean and degrease the surface and help the paint adhere.

If you have to add new hinges or hardware to an antique or antique-looking piece of furniture, you can make the hinges look more aged by blotting them with vinegar and letting it sit for 24 hours. Repeat until you achieve desired effect.

Odors

When applying new paint of any kind, keep small dishes of vinegar around the room to absorb paint odors. Keep dishes out for a few days, adding new vinegar each day.

If your paint project is going to take a while, try this method to eliminate paint odors: Fill a bucket with hay, and drizzle vinegar over hay. Let it stand for 15 minutes, then cover hay with water.

Paintbrushes

Soften paint-hardened paintbrushes by soaking them for an hour in warm vinegar. First boil the vinegar, then pour enough into a container to cover bristles. Do not let sit longer than a few hours or bristles may be ruined. Wash brushes afterward in soap and water, then allow to air dry before using.

Windows

When trying to remove dried paint on glass windows, first spray the paint with warm vinegar, then carefully scrape or peel off paint.

Removing Wallpaper

To strip glued-on wallpaper, first remove all that you can by just pulling it off. Next add undiluted vinegar to a spray bottle, and spray stripped areas until they are very damp but not running. Let sit for 5 minutes, then find an edge and pull away. Wipe any remaining glue residue off wall using vinegar on a cloth or sponge. Heating the vinegar first may speed up this process and help remove the most stubborn strips.

Wall Recovery

Adhesives

Remove self-adhesive hooks or other sticky accessories from a plaster wall by dripping vinegar behind the base of the accessory. Let vinegar soak in a few minutes, then peel away.

Apply a dishcloth soaked in hot vinegar to a decal stuck on a wall or wood surface. You may need to use masking tape to attach dishcloth to sticky area. Let sit for 5 minutes, then remove dishcloth and peel off decal.

Plaster

Add ½ teaspoon vinegar to 1 quart patching plastic to extend the amount of time you have to work with the plaster before it hardens.

Homemade Plaster

Mix 2 tablespoons cornstarch and 2 tablespoons salt, then add enough water (about 5 teaspoons) to make a thick paste. Use paste to fill a small nail hole, chip, or other hole in sheetrock or plaster. Let dry, then sand lightly and paint.

Wood Repair

Furniture

If you're trying to take apart a piece of furniture, you can dissolve the old glue by applying warm vinegar to it. Drip vinegar directly onto furniture joints using an eyedropper. Let vinegar soak in, then carefully pry joints apart.

Tighten up the sagging seat of a cane chair by sponging it with a 50/50 solution of vinegar and water. Set chair out in the sun to dry.

Scratches and blisters

Combine an equal amount of vinegar and iodine, then apply mixture to a scratch in wood using an artist's paintbrush. If you need a deep color, add a little more iodine; for lighter colors, add more vinegar.

Spots and stains

Use coarse steel wool dipped in mineral spirits to scrub a stain on a wood floor. After scrubbing, wipe with vinegar on a scrubbing sponge. Allow vinegar to penetrate, then repeat and rinse if necessary.

Dark spots sometimes appear on wood floors where an alkaline substance has dripped and dried. To remove spot, first strip floor of any wax using mineral spirits on a cloth. Next apply white vinegar to spotted area and leave on for 5 minutes. Wipe dry, and repeat if spot remains. If several applications don't remove spot, consult a professional floor finisher.

A varnish finish on wood can sometimes become clouded and tired-looking. Spruce it up by rubbing

Healing Blisters

A blister on a veneer surface can be repaired by carefully cutting a slit at the edge of the blister where the veneer is still glued to the underlying surface. Be sure to follow the grain of the wood when cutting. Hold split open with the tip of a knife, then fill hollow blister with warm vinegar. Let it stand for several hours to dissolve glue. Wipe away any excess vinegar, and let blistered area dry overnight. Work wood glue under blister, then apply pressure and flatten out area.

area with a soft cloth dipped in a mixture of 1 tablespoon vinegar to 1 quart water. Dry with a second soft cloth.

Customized Wood Stain

Mix white vinegar with any water-base ink to create your very own wood stain. The vinegar gives colored ink a silvery sheen. To make, pour a small amount of vinegar into a container, then add ink until desired color is achieved. Apply stain to unfinished wood with a brush or rag, the same way you would any other stain. Wipe off excess.

More Household Repair Hints and Tips

Candles

Stop new candles from dripping by first soaking them in a strong solution of ½ cup water and ½ cup salt for several hours. Let dry, then burn as usual.

Fireplaces

An occasional handful of salt thrown into your fireplace fire will help loosen soot inside your chimney. It also makes a cheery, bright yellow flame.

Grease

Sponge away grease and dirt on your stove's exhaust fan and your air conditioner blades with pure vinegar. This will help prevent dust buildup.

Do You Need Softer Water?

Sometimes household water can be too hard to do an effective job of cleaning. The water supply contains high concentrations of the minerals calcium and magnesium because of the geology and source of water in that region. One way to determine if you have hard water is if your soap and laundry detergent don't lather very well or your glasses and dishes are left with significant water spots after running them through the dishwasher. Also, your bathtub and bath fixtures may develop a filmy feel.

A household water softener works to take calcium and magnesium out of the water supply, but this wouldn't work without the addition of water softener salts, which are pellets of sodium that absorb the hardening minerals and keep the softener running efficiently.

Knives

Before sharpening knives with a whetstone, first dampen whetstone with vinegar.

Propane lamps

Soak the casing of a propane lamp in vinegar. Let dry completely before using. This will help the lamp give off more light and extend the length of time it burns.

Rust

Remove rust from nuts, bolts, or nails by placing them in a glass jar, covering them with vinegar, sealing the jar, and letting them sit overnight.

Rusty tools can be revived in the same manner. Soak them in pure vinegar for several hours, then rub away rust. Change vinegar if it becomes cloudy before rust is softened.

Another rust removal method is to make a paste of lemon juice and salt. Apply paste to rusted object, and rub with a dry, soft cloth.

Mix salt and cream of tartar, and moisten with enough water to make a paste. Apply to a rust stain on a piece of metal outdoor furniture; let sit in the sun until dry. Repeat if necessary.

Septic tanks

If your home uses a septic tank rather than a city septic system, you want to be careful about how you clean your toilet. Harsh chemicals flushed down the toilet could harm your tank. Instead, use vinegar to clean it by adding 1 gallon to the toilet bowl. Let sit 1 hour, then brush and flush.

Salt Snippet

Wit is the salt of conversation, not the food.

—William Hazlitt

Chapter 4

Laundry

Salt is a super stain remover on clothing, while vinegar is a veritable powerhouse when it comes to pretreating stains, softening water, and boosting regular laundry detergents. When cleaning fabrics, white or distilled vinegar is preferred, but apple cider vinegar works just as well if that's what you have on hand. *Please note:* None of the tips listed here should be tried with dry-clean-only fabrics.

The Basics

Blankets

When washing cotton or washable wool blankets, add 2 cups vinegar to rinse cycle. This will help remove soap and make blankets soft and fluffy.

Clothes softener

Add ½ cup vinegar to rinse cycle of your wash to soften clothes.

Color bleeding

Prevent colors from bleeding by adding 1 cup white vinegar to the wash along with laundry detergent.

Add ½ cup salt to wash cycle to prevent new colored fabrics from running.

Lint

Reduce lint buildup and keep pet hair from clinging to clothing by adding vinegar to rinse cycle.

New clothes

Some new clothes may be treated with a chemical that can be irritating to sensitive skin. Before wearing anything new, soak it in 1 gallon water with ½ cup vinegar. Rinse, then wash as usual.

Static cling

A good way to control static cling is to add ½ cup vinegar to last rinse cycle of your wash.

Special Care for Special Fabrics

Delicates

If washing delicate items by hand, follow garment's care instructions, and add 1 or 2 tablespoons vinegar to last rinse to help remove soap residue.

Leather

Clean leather with a mixture of 1 cup boiled linseed oil and 1 cup white vinegar. Carefully apply to any spots with a soft cloth. Let dry.

Silk

Dip silks (do not soak) in a mixture of ½ cup mild detergent and 2 tablespoons white vinegar to 2 quarts cold water. Rinse well, then roll in a heavy towel to soak up excess moisture. Iron while still damp.

Keep Colors Colorful

Brighten the colors of washable curtains or fiber rugs by washing them in a saltwater solution.

Faded rugs and carpets can be brightened with a brisk rub by a cloth dampened with a strong saltwater solution.

Any colored clothing item that has become dulled can be brightened by soaking it in 1 gallon warm water and 1 cup white vinegar. Follow this with a clear water rinse.

Yellowing

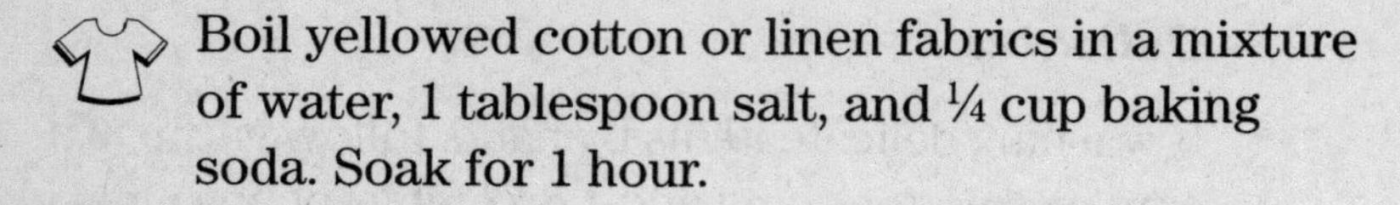

Boil yellowed cotton or linen fabrics in a mixture of water, 1 tablespoon salt, and ¼ cup baking soda. Soak for 1 hour.

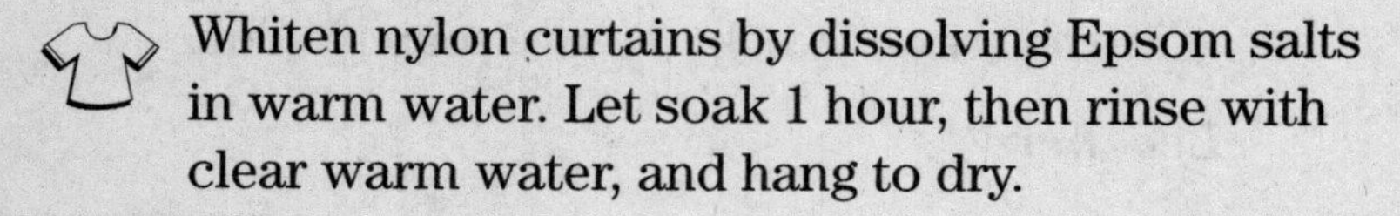

Whiten nylon curtains by dissolving Epsom salts in warm water. Let soak 1 hour, then rinse with clear warm water, and hang to dry.

When hand washing linen, wool, or silk, prevent them from yellowing by adding ½ cup vinegar to rinse water.

Ironing out the Rough Spots

Cleaning

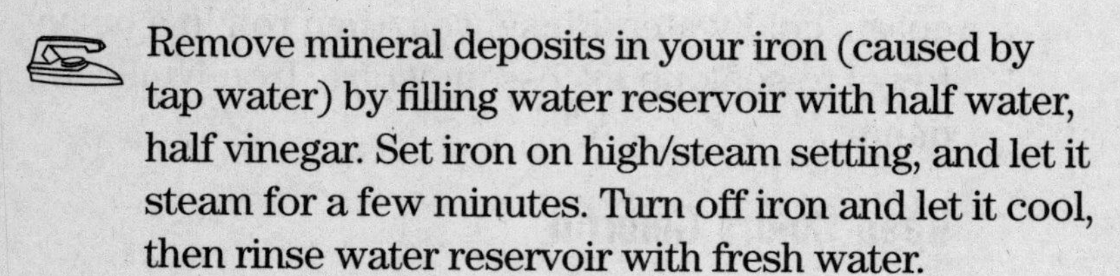

Remove mineral deposits in your iron (caused by tap water) by filling water reservoir with half water, half vinegar. Set iron on high/steam setting, and let it steam for a few minutes. Turn off iron and let it cool, then rinse water reservoir with fresh water.

An iron with rough or sticky spots on its surface can be cleaned by running it, set at low, over a piece of paper with salt on it.

Creases

To remove a crease in knit fabrics, dip a cloth in a solution of ⅓ distilled vinegar and ⅔ water, then use the cloth to crease. Place a brown paper bag over crease, and iron.

The Problem of Perspiration

Don't despair. Those yellow stains in the armpits and around the collar of your favorite white T-shirts aren't a sign that you're sweating too much or not cleaning properly. These areas are just harder to get clean and are made up of more than just old perspiration and dirt. Undissolved deodorants may be a culprit, too. If you have hard water, the deodorant residue (and soap and perspiration) can't wash out properly. Below are methods for removing perspiration stains. You may have to experiment, depending on the fabric and age of the stain, to see which one works best for you.

Mix 1 quart water with 4 tablespoons salt. Sponge this mixture onto stained area, then repeat until stain disappears.

For older perspiration stains, soak area in undiluted vinegar. Let it sit 15 to 20 minutes, then launder as usual.

Treat ring around the collar with a paste of baking soda and ¼ cup water. Rub in and let it sit 10 minutes, then add enough vinegar to dampen area. Wash as usual.

Rub a paste of vinegar and baking soda into collar grime using a toothbrush. Saturate and let sit before laundering.

Starch

Add a dash of salt to laundry starch to keep iron from sticking to clothing. This will also help give a smooth finish to linens or fine cottons.

Control Clothes Odor

Bleach

Clothes that have been bleached may retain an unpleasant bleach smell. Lightly spray item with a mixture of ¼ cup vinegar to ¾ cup water, or rinse it again in washing machine with 1 cup vinegar added to load.

Pet urine

Add ½ to 1 cup vinegar to a wash load, and run cycle as usual.

Smoke

Remove smoke odors from clothing by filling a bathtub with very hot water and 1 cup vinegar. Hang clothes above tub in the steam.

A Guide to Stain Removal

Blood

Soak a bloodstain in cotton, linen, or other natural fiber in cold saltwater for 1 hour. Wash using warm water and laundry soap, then boil fabric in a large kettle of boiling water. Wash again.

A fresh bloodstain should disappear easily if it is immediately covered with salt and blotted with cold water. Keep adding fresh water and blotting until stain is gone.

Coffee and tea

For coffee or tea stains that have set, soak item in a solution of ⅓ cup vinegar to ⅔ cup water, then hang in the sun to dry.

Brand-new coffee or tea drips should easily be removed with lots of cold water on a damp cloth if fabric is not dry-clean-only.

Grass

Removal of severe grass stains on white clothes can be helped along by soaking in full-strength vinegar for a half hour before washing.

Gravy

Try covering a fresh gravy stain with salt and letting it absorb as much of the grease as possible. A stubborn stain may need a 50/50 solution of ammonia and vinegar dabbed on and blotted until stain disappears.

Grease

Remove a fresh grease spot on fabric by covering it with salt. Wait for salt to absorb grease, then gently brush salt away. Repeat until spot is gone, then launder as usual.

Double-knit fabrics can be a special stain challenge when it comes to grease. Add ½ teaspoon salt to a small dish of ammonia, and dab mixture directly onto grease spot. Let sit, then wash as usual.

Gum

If sticky spots remain after removing a piece of gum from clothing, soak spot in vinegar for 10 to 15 minutes. Launder as usual.

Ink

Rub salt onto a fresh ink stain on fabric, and soak fabric overnight in milk. Wash as usual.

An older ink stain in cotton fabric may be helped by spraying with hair spray. Dab with vinegar to remove sticky spray.

Juice

Dried-on red berry juice may be removed from bleach-safe garments by soaking in a solution of ⅓ vinegar and ⅔ water. Wash as usual.

Mildew

Make a thin paste of lemon juice and salt, then spread paste on mildew stains. Lay clothing item out in the sun to bleach it, then rinse and dry.

A mixture of salt, vinegar, and water should remove mildew stains on most fabrics. Use up to full-strength vinegar if mildew is extensive.

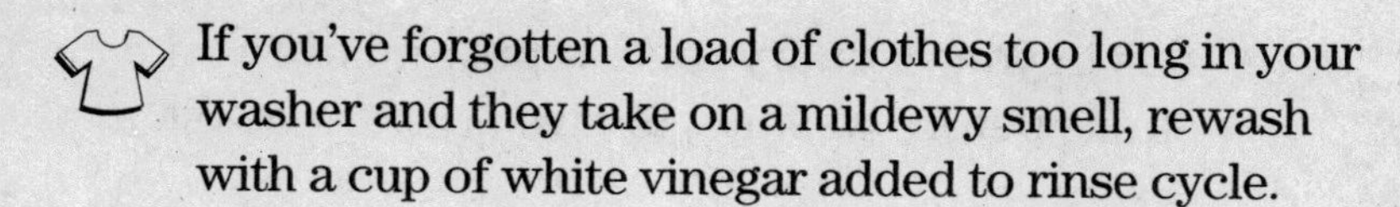

If you've forgotten a load of clothes too long in your washer and they take on a mildewy smell, rewash with a cup of white vinegar added to rinse cycle.

Remove mildew stains and other soils from shower curtains, even plastic ones, by machine washing them with 2 bath towels. Add 1 cup white vinegar to rinse cycle, and tumble dry.

Prevent mildew growth on shower curtains by soaking them in a bathtub full of saltwater (½ cup salt to the tub). Soak for several hours, then hang to dry.

Keep a spray bottle of vinegar in your shower area, and use it to spritz shower curtains occasionally just after showering. This treatment should help control mildew development.

Pretreatment

For synthetic blends or old stains on natural materials, presoak stain in ammonia before applying vinegar and water.

Tough Stain Remover

Keep this pretreatment solution on hand in the laundry room to use on virtually all tough clothing stains. Just combine ½ cup vinegar, ½ cup ammonia, ½ cup baking soda, 2 squirts liquid soap, and 2 quarts water. Keep solution in a clearly labeled spray bottle.

A basic mixture of half water and half vinegar as a laundry pretreatment can do the trick with many common stains on clothing. Keep a spray bottle of this in your laundry room. Spray mixture on stains before washing to give an extra boost.

Suede

Remove grease from suede by dipping a cloth in vinegar and gently sponging stain. Let dry completely, then use a fine brush to restore nap in suede.

Wine

Remove a wine spill from cotton fabrics by immediately sprinkling stained area with enough salt to soak up liquid. Then soak fabric for 1 hour in cold water, and launder as usual.

More Laundry Hints and Tips

Baby items

Take special care when washing baby clothes by always using 1 cup vinegar in rinse water to remove soap residue and break down uric acid.

Help keep wool and cotton baby blankets soft and fluffy by adding 2 cups vinegar to rinse water during wash cycle.

A cup of vinegar added to rinse cycle when washing baby clothes will help eliminate odors and soften clothing.

Before washings, cloth baby diapers should be kept in a diaper pail with 1 cup vinegar and

2 gallons water or a similar ratio for small containers. This will neutralize urine and help prevent stains.

Using vinegar in rinse cycle of a load of diapers may help prevent diaper rash among babies who use cloth diapers. It also helps remove harsh bleaches or detergents and soften the fabric.

Rust-removing Treatment

Make a thin paste of vinegar and salt, then spread paste on rust stains in fabric. Lay item out in the sun to bleach it, or apply paste, stretch fabric over a large kettle, and pour boiling water through stained area. In both cases, allow item to dry, then check stain. Run item through rinse cycle in washing machine, then check stain again. Repeat treatment if any stain remains.

Pantyhose

When hand washing nylon pantyhose, add 1 tablespoon vinegar to rinse water to help make them last longer.

To make pantyhose more resistant to running, wash and dry a new pair as you normally would. Then soak hose in 1 gallon water with 2 cups salt added. Totally immerse pantyhose, and soak them for 3 hours. Rinse in cool water; drip dry.

Setting dye

Add a cup of distilled vinegar to last rinse water when dying fabrics. This will help set the color.

Shoes and boots

Clean the salt residue common on winter boots with a cloth dipped in a solution of 1 cup water and 1 tablespoon vinegar. This will work on leather and vinyl boots and shoes.

Use a soft cloth dipped in vinegar to shine a pair of patent-leather shoes or any patent-leather item.

Sneakers or any shoes that are starting to smell can be helped by sprinkling with a little salt. Let sit overnight. The salt will help control moisture, which contributes to odors.

Washing machine

Soap, mineral deposits, and wet lint can build up inside your washer, reducing its efficiency or even causing it to malfunction. Clean machine once a year by filling it with hot water and then adding a quart of white vinegar (or more, depending on how dirty machine is). Run machine through its normal wash and rinse cycle.

You can also clean your washing machine and its hoses by dumping a gallon of distilled vinegar into the tub and running machine through an entire wash cycle.

If your washing machine has a removable filter, clean it by using an old toothbrush to remove any lint. Then soak filter in vinegar overnight, and rinse it with water.

Chapter 5

Beauty and Relaxation

Vinegar and salt solutions are wonderful—and inexpensive—additions to your beauty and stress-reduction regimens. Vinegar can help restore the natural acidity of your skin, which may clear up skin problems such as dryness, itchiness, flakiness, and acne, while salt added to warm water has a softening effect on skin. Read on for even more beauty tips and tricks that will help you stay relaxed and beautiful without spending a fortune.

Body Beautiful

Age spots

Vinegar mixed with onion juice may help reduce the appearance of age spots. Mix equal parts onion juice and vinegar, and dab onto age spots. After several weeks of this daily routine, spots should lighten.

Exfoliation

After you take a shower or bath and while your skin is still wet, sprinkle salt onto your hands and rub it all over your skin. This salt massage will remove dry skin and make your skin smoother to the touch. It will also invigorate your skin and get your circulation moving. Try it first thing in the morning to help wake up or after a period of physical exertion.

Itchy skin

Soaking in a tub of saltwater can be a great itchy skin reliever. Just add 1 cup table salt or sea salt to bath water. This solution will also soften skin and relax you.

To relieve itchy skin and/or aching muscles, add 8 ounces apple cider vinegar to a bathtub of warm water. Soak in tub for at least 15 minutes.

Vinegar Vignette

Whoever loses his hair should pound up peach kernels, mix them with vinegar and put them on the bald place.

—Folk wisdom

Put on a Happy Face

Aftershave

Apple cider vinegar is a great aftershave for men that will help keep their skin soft and young-looking. Keep a small bottle of it in the medicine cabinet, and splash on face after shaving.

Cleansers and toners

Use a mixture of half vinegar, half water to clean your face. Then rinse with vinegar diluted with water, and let face air dry to seal in moisture.

Herb-scented Skin Toner

Use 1 part vinegar to 3 parts water, and add the following flower or herb petals of your choice. Spray on skin as desired to freshen.

For dry skin: **violet, rose, borage, or jasmine**

For oily skin: **peppermint, marigold, rosemary, or lavender**

For sensitive skin: **violet, salt burnet, parsley, or borage**

For normal skin: **lemon balm, rose, spearmint, or chamomile**

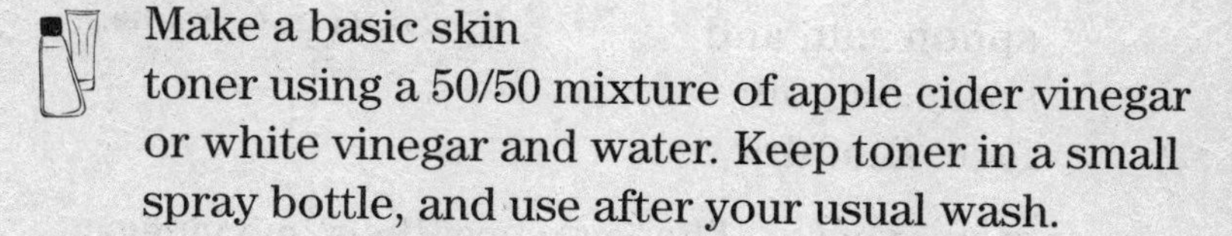

Make a basic skin toner using a 50/50 mixture of apple cider vinegar or white vinegar and water. Keep toner in a small spray bottle, and use after your usual wash.

Mix 1 teaspoon salt and 1 teaspoon olive oil in a small bowl, then use mixture to gently massage face and throat. Follow by washing with your usual face soap; rinse.

Problem skin

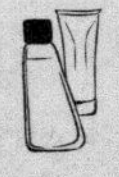

Oily skin can be controlled with a mixture of half apple cider vinegar and half cool water. The mixture works as an astringent. You can also freeze this solution into ice cubes and use it as a cooling facial treatment on a hot summer day.

Another oily skin treatment is to put tepid water into a small spray bottle, add 1 teaspoon salt, and spray on your face. Blot dry.

Acne Treatment

Use a clean travel-size bottle to mix 1 teaspoon vinegar and 10 teaspoons water. Clean your face as usual in the morning, then carry this bottle and a few cotton balls with you so you can dab acne spots several times during the day. This solution shouldn't dry out your skin, and the vinegar will help return your skin to a natural pH balance. The treatment may also help prevent future acne outbreaks. Discontinue use if irritation worsens.

Make a paste of honey, wheat flour, and vinegar, then use it to lightly cover a new outbreak of pimples. Keep paste on overnight, and rinse off in the morning. This should enhance the healing process.

Facial Splashes

Herbal: **Boil 1 quart apple cider vinegar in microwave for 3 minutes in a large glass measuring cup. Remove and add herbs (lavender or rosemary are excellent). Pour into a sterilized bottle.**

Mint: **Bruise a handful of mint leaves by rolling them with a pastry rolling pin. Pack them into a jar, and cover with apple cider vinegar. Let stand 2 weeks, then strain out mint. Pour remaining liquid in an empty, clean jar.**

Rosewater: **Mix the following in a jar: 1 pint apple cider vinegar, 1 ounce rose petals, ½ pint rosewater, ½ pint vinegar, and 1 ounce aromatic flowers such as sweet violet, rosemary, or lavender. Steep for 2 weeks, then strain. Pour remaining liquid in an empty, clean jar.**

For Sweet Breath and Clean Teeth

Dentures

To brighten dentures, soak them overnight in pure white vinegar.

Mouthwash

Mix ½ teaspoon salt and ½ teaspoon baking soda into a 4-ounce glass of water. Use this solution to gargle and freshen breath.

Another refreshing mouthwash can be made with ¼ cup water and ¼ cup vinegar in a 4-ounce glass. Gargle with this to freshen your mouth and control bad breath.

Toothpaste

A mixture of salt and baking soda makes an excellent toothpaste that can help whiten teeth and remove plaque, which contributes to cavities and gum disease. To make, pulverize salt in a blender or food processor, or spread some on a cutting board and roll it with a pastry rolling pin to crush salt into a fine sandlike texture. Mix 1 part crushed salt with 2 parts baking soda, then dip a dampened toothbrush into mixture and brush teeth. Keep powder in an airtight container in your bathroom.

Help Your Hands

Chapped

Mix equal parts vinegar and hand cream to help chapped hands.

Nail polish

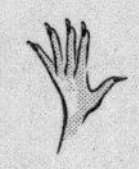

Make your nail polish last longer on your fingers by soaking fingertips for 1 minute in 2 teaspoons vinegar and ½ cup warm water before applying polish.

Odors

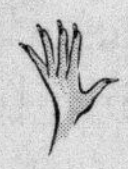

To remove onion odor from your hands, sprinkle on a little salt, then moisten with a bit of vinegar. Rub hands together, and rinse.

Scrub

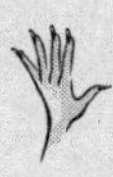

Clean very dirty hands by scrubbing with cornmeal that has been moistened with a little bit of apple cider vinegar. Rinse in cool water, then dry.

Softer Hands

Combine 1 gallon white distilled vinegar and herbs and spices like cinnamon, nutmeg, or cardamom. Let mixture sit for 1 month, then strain out spice or herb debris. Pour the fragrant vinegar into an empty, clean bottle with a spray nozzle, or buy a new decorative bottle to keep at your sink. After you wash dishes or when you've had your hands in hot water, spray vinegar mixture on your hands. Regular use of this vinegar spray will soften your hands and make them smell nice, too!

Fix Your Feet

Aches

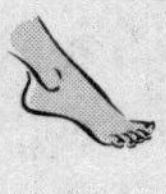

Relieve aching and tired feet by soaking them in a tub of warm salt water. Just add a handful of salt to a gallon of water in a plastic dishpan, and soak feet for a half hour or more.

Add 1½ gallons warm water to a large plastic basin, then mix in ¼ cup salt and ¼ cup baking soda. Soak feet for 15 minutes.

Corns and calluses

Help remove corns and calluses by covering rough areas with cotton balls that have been soaked in vinegar. Secure cotton balls with tape or bandages; leave on overnight. The area should be softened by morning. Repeat this procedure until problem areas disappear.

Get Rid of Athlete's Foot

Relieve athlete's foot by soaking feet every night in pure vinegar for 10 minutes. (This may sting if skin is broken. Discontinue soaking if irritation continues.) After soaking feet, soak a pair of socks in a mixture of 1 part water and 1 part vinegar. Wear the wet socks on affected feet for at least 30 minutes. Remove, and pat feet dry. Repeat this procedure daily until condition improves.

Odor

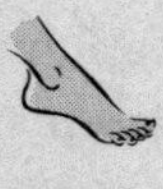

To control foot odor, soak feet in a mixture of 1 gallon warm water and 1 ounce vinegar.

Healthy Hair

Conditioning

Vinegar is a great hair conditioner and can improve cleanliness and shine. For simple conditioning, just add 1 tablespoon vinegar to your hair as you rinse it. Keep a travel-size plastic bottle of this mixture in your shower for this purpose.

Dandruff

Massage full-strength vinegar into your scalp several times a week before shampooing. This can help create healthy hair and control dandruff.

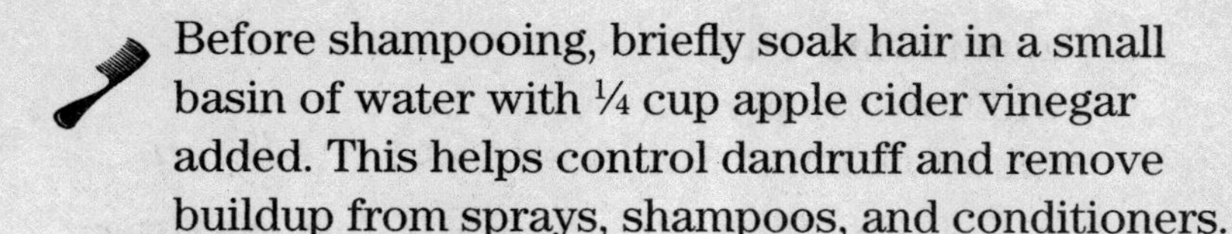

Before shampooing, briefly soak hair in a small basin of water with ¼ cup apple cider vinegar added. This helps control dandruff and remove buildup from sprays, shampoos, and conditioners.

To control dandruff, mix 2 cups water and ½ cup vinegar, and use this to rinse after shampooing. If you need a stronger treatment for dandruff control, use this same method, but keep rinse on your hair for 1 hour, covered with a shower cap. Rinse. This mixture will also help control frizziness in dry or damaged hair.

Hair Conditioning Treatment

Give your hair a conditioning treatment that will leave it feeling like you've been to an expensive salon.

Mix together 3 eggs, 2 tablespoons olive oil or safflower oil, and 1 teaspoon vinegar, then apply to hair. Cover with a plastic cap, and leave on for a half hour. Shampoo as usual.

Gray

Use 1 tablespoon apple cider vinegar in 1 gallon water as an after-shampoo rinse that will minimize gray in your hair.

More Beauty and Relaxation Hints and Tips

Deodorant

Make a homemade deodorant by combining equal amounts of water and vinegar and dabbing lightly under arms. This will not stop perspiration, but it will control odor.

Eye puffiness

To get rid of puffy eyes that can accompany allergies, colds, crying, or lack of sleep, mix 1 teaspoon salt into 1 pint hot water. Dip cotton balls or facial pads into solution, then lie down and apply pads to eyelids. Rest quietly in this position for at least 15 minutes, keeping pads in place. Eyes should be back to normal when you sit up.

Cover the Gray

This hair rinse can cover gray and treat dandruff at the same time.

Combine 2 cups fresh sage and 1 cup fresh rosemary leaves in a pan, then add just enough water to cover the herbs. Bring mixture to a boil. Simmer for 6 hours, taking care not to let all the water boil away. Remove from heat, and let mixture steep overnight. Strain, then add enough water to make 5 cups. Add 2 teaspoons apple cider vinegar, and store in a plastic bottle. To use, thoroughly rub mixture into scalp, then lightly rinse.

Eyeglass cleaner

Clean your glasses with a drop of vinegar and a soft cloth.

Chapter 6

Home Remedies

Scurvy, cholera, diphtheria, high fever, dysentery, urinary infections, scarlatina, tonsillitis, hoarseness, external inflammations, contusions, joint injuries, apathy, obesity, hay fever, asthma, rashes, food poisoning, heartburn, bad eyesight, brittle nails, bad breath—this is just a sampling of all the ailments for which vinegar has been prescribed. Modern science doesn't endorse most of these ideas today, but this list offers a picture of the seemingly endless healing qualities vinegar may have.

Aches, Pains, and Strains

Backaches

Soaking in a bathtub of hot water and 2 cups vinegar for 30 minutes will greatly relieve a minor backache and soothe sore muscles.

Bursitis

Boil 1 cup apple cider vinegar, and add 1 teaspoon cayenne pepper during boil. Cool this mixture, then apply it in a compress to affected area. Make sure cayenne doesn't irritate the skin. The compress should make the area feel warm but not burning.

Headache

Ease a headache by lying down and applying a compress dipped in a mixture of half warm water and half vinegar to the temples.

Use above treatment for treating a headache, but try an herbal vinegar such as lavender to provide aromatic relief.

Leg cramps

Ease the pain of a leg cramp or other cramp in the body by using a soft cloth soaked in full-strength vinegar as a compress.

Homemade Liniment

Blend 1 egg, slightly beaten; 1 cup vinegar; and 1 cup turpentine, and apply mixture to sprained area. Discard immediately after use.

Muscle sprain

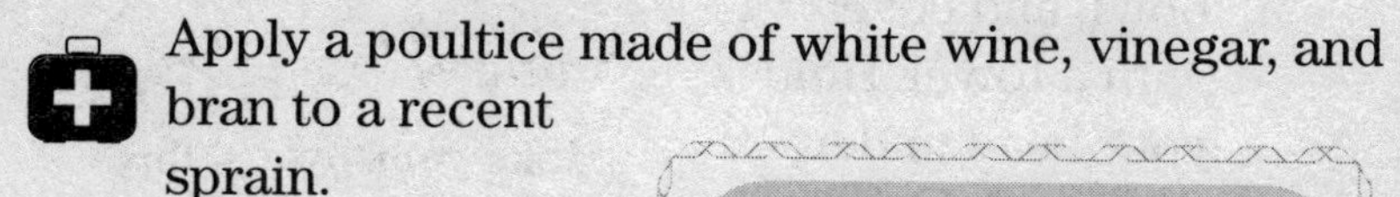

Apply a poultice made of white wine, vinegar, and bran to a recent sprain.

Use a towel soaked in hot vinegar as a compress to ease the pain of a recent muscle strain or sprain. Apply for only 20 minutes at a time. If pain persists, consult a physician.

Homemade Cough Syrup

During a period of cold or flu, make your own cough syrup to have on hand. Mix ¼ cup honey and ¼ cup apple cider vinegar, and pour into a jar or bottle that can be tightly sealed. Shake well before each use. Take 1 tablespoon every 4 hours. If cough persists for more than a week, see a physician.

It's Flu Season!

Cough

Sprinkle your pillowcase with apple cider vinegar to control nighttime coughing.

Respiratory congestion

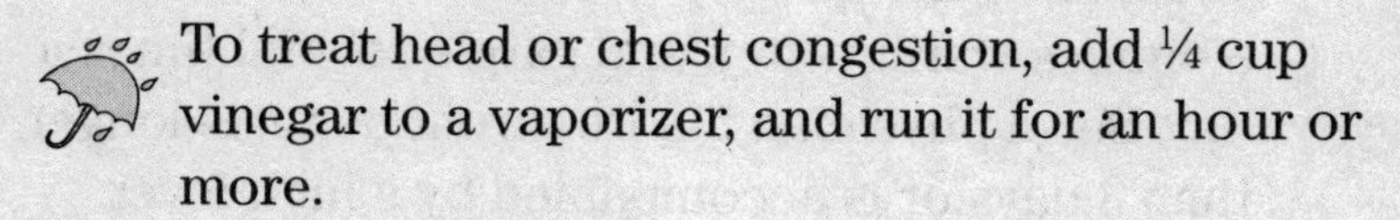

To treat head or chest congestion, add ¼ cup vinegar to a vaporizer, and run it for an hour or more.

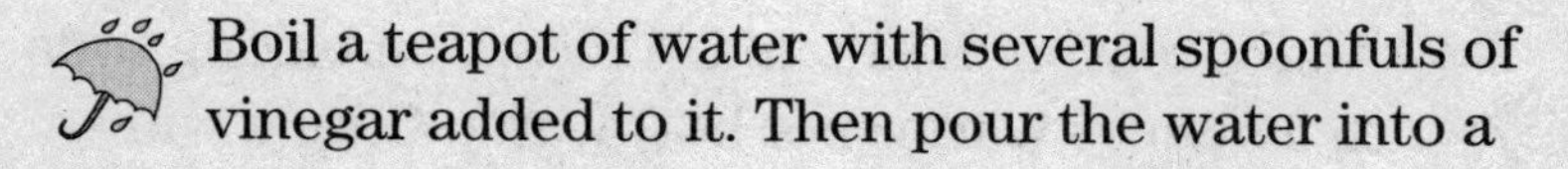

Boil a teapot of water with several spoonfuls of vinegar added to it. Then pour the water into a dishpan or large bowl, and cover with a towel. Hold your head under the towel, breathing in steam, to help loosen chest congestion.

Sinus congestion

Breathing in steam from a vaporizer can be beneficial in treating the facial pain of a sinus infection. Add ¼ cup vinegar to vaporizer, and breathe in deeply.

Saline Nose Drops

Make your own saline drops to use for controlling annoying post-nasal drip. People with sleep apnea, a condition that involves a dangerous interruption of breathing while asleep, may also want to try these drops to help keep nasal passages open.

Mix ¼ teaspoon salt and ¼ teaspoon baking soda into 8 ounces boiled water. Draw liquid into an eyedropper, then apply to both nostrils with head tilted back. Hold this position for 15 seconds, then blow nose.

Sore throat

The simplest remedy for minor sore throat pain is a warm saltwater gargle (no matter how much you dislike the taste!). Just add 1 teaspoon salt to 8 ounces warm water, and gargle several times a day. See a physician if sore throat persists longer than 3 days or is accompanied by a high fever.

Add ¼ teaspoon salt and ¼ teaspoon baking soda to 8 ounces warm (not hot) water. Gargle with mixture 3 times a day to ease sore throat. If pain persists longer than 3 days, see a physician.

Vinegar can also be used for a sore throat. Use 1 teaspoon per 8 ounces of water, and gargle.

To ease a sore throat and to thin mucus, gargle with undiluted apple cider vinegar that has a little salt and pepper added to it.

Allergy Treatment

Irrigating the nostrils and sinuses with saltwater is an excellent way to control persistent, annoying allergy symptoms. Dissolve ½ teaspoon salt in 8 ounces room-temperature water. Draw mixture into a nose dropper, and breath in the liquid through your nostrils. Repeat several times for each nostril, using 2 or 3 drops of solution each time. When through, blow nose until no discharge remains.

Oral Dilemmas

Burns or injuries

A severe burn in your mouth from eating something very hot (cheese is often a culprit!) can be relieved by rinsing with saltwater every hour or so. Use ½ teaspoon salt in 8 ounces warm water.

Biting the tongue or cheek can result in a large amount of blood but is rarely serious. To ease the pain, rinse mouth with 1 teaspoon salt in 1 cup warm water.

Gums

Use 1 teaspoon salt to 4 ounces warm water to swish with when gums are painful. If you have an abscess, the salt will draw out some of the infection. Any gum pain should be treated by a dentist as soon as possible.

Toothaches

As a temporary remedy for a toothache before you can get to the dentist, rinse your mouth with a mixture of 4 ounces warm water, 2 tablespoons vinegar, and 1 tablespoon salt.

Two to 3 teaspoons salt in warm water will also help relieve the pain of a sore tooth.

When Summer's Not Fun

Bee stings and bug bites

Work a mixture of salt and water into a paste that will stick to a bee sting or bug bite. Apply paste; let sit until dry. This should relieve any itch or pain.

Use vinegar mixed with cornstarch to make a paste. Apply paste to a bee sting or bug bite, and let dry.

Combine equal parts baking soda and salt, then brush onto a sting or bite area to help relieve itch.

Treat a mosquito bite by soaking it in salt water, then applying an ointment made of salt and lard.

Poison ivy and poison oak

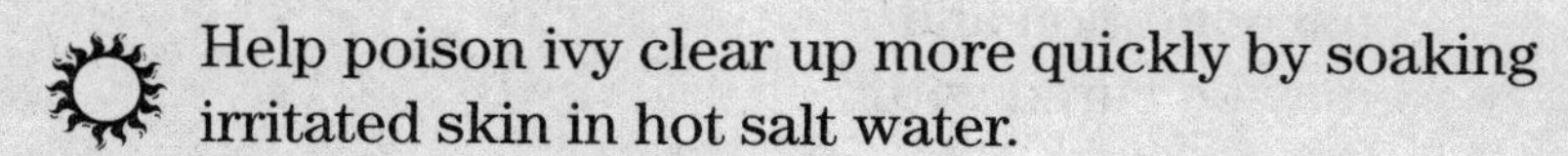

Help poison ivy clear up more quickly by soaking irritated skin in hot salt water.

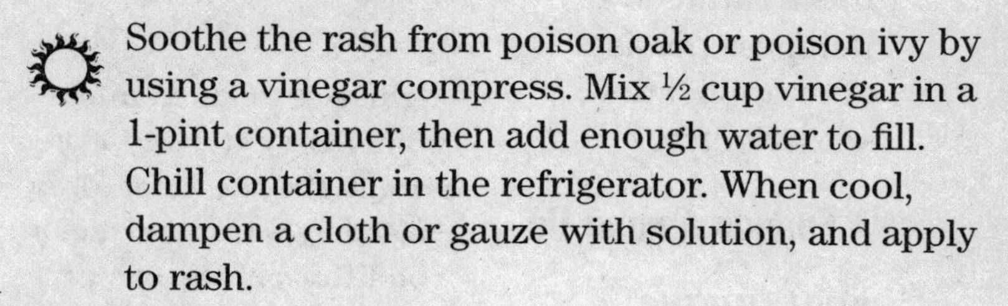

Soothe the rash from poison oak or poison ivy by using a vinegar compress. Mix ½ cup vinegar in a 1-pint container, then add enough water to fill. Chill container in the refrigerator. When cool, dampen a cloth or gauze with solution, and apply to rash.

Sunburn

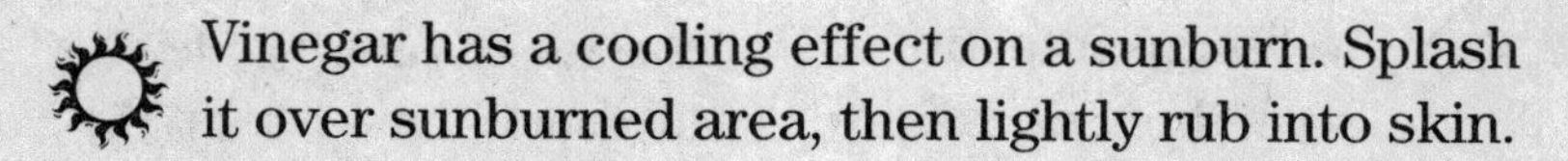

Vinegar has a cooling effect on a sunburn. Splash it over sunburned area, then lightly rub into skin.

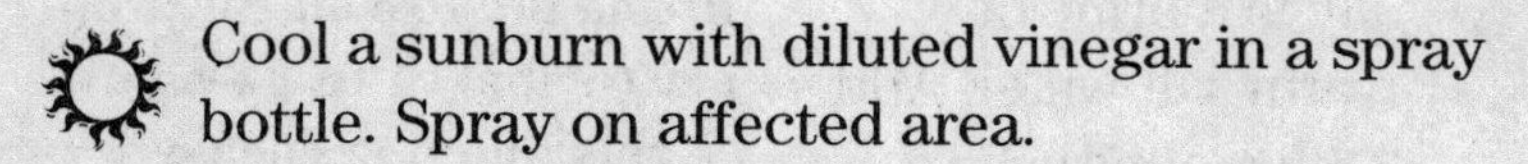

Cool a sunburn with diluted vinegar in a spray bottle. Spray on affected area.

The Skinny on Skin Problems

Burns

For a minor burn, cover it with a piece of cloth or gauze that has been soaked in chilled vinegar. This will control the pain. Repeat twice an hour if pain persists. Do not use this on any burn where skin is broken.

Irritation

Pharmacists have recommended vinegar to customers complaining of skin ailments. If an irritated area stops itching after applying vinegar, it is probably an external condition and may be cured with this treatment. If itchiness persists after application, see a doctor.

A Fungus Among Us

Foot fungus

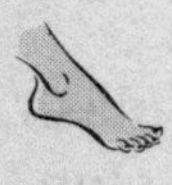

If your feet are prone to fungus infections, soak them occasionally in a brine of warm salt water. Add 2 teaspoons salt to 1 gallon water, and soak for 5 to 10 minutes. This treatment will soften callused areas and will also help control foot odor.

Toe fungus

Saturate toenails plagued by fungus with a cotton ball that has been soaked in a 50/50 mixture of warm water and vinegar. Attach cotton ball to problem area and let

Relief for Swimmer's Ear

Swimmer's ear, an infection of the exterior of the ear and the ear canal often caused by water and damp conditions in the ear, can be treated with vinegar.

Combine ¼ cup vinegar and ¼ cup rubbing alcohol in a small jar with a tight-fitting lid. Use an ear dropper to apply 1 to 2 drops of this liquid in each ear 3 times a day during swimming season to prevent infection. This solution may also prevent other types of ear infections. Do not use this treatment if you suspect an inner-ear infection; instead, see a doctor as soon as possible.

sit until cotton dries out. Repeat nightly until condition improves. If you don't see a change after 6 weeks, see a physician. Fungal infections are persistent and prone to recurrence, so be sure to wash and dry hands thoroughly after contact with any fungal infection.

Head Lice

Vinegar can help control an infestation of head lice. First use a medicated head lice shampoo, or follow your doctor's instructions for lice control. After shampooing hair, rinse with white vinegar, and go through hair with a comb dipped in vinegar. The vinegar will help loosen any remaining nits, or eggs, from hair. Continue with treatment prescribed on shampoo bottle.

More Home Remedies

Hemorrhoids

Use a cotton ball dipped in vinegar to soothe the pain and itch associated with hemorrhoids. If area is irritated, the vinegar may sting, so try a diluted solution.

Incontinence

A person prone to having urinary accidents is also at risk for developing irritated skin from the wetness. Always clean damp areas with soap and water followed by a rinse of diluted vinegar to disinfect and control odors.

Nosebleed

When experiencing a minor nosebleed, apply a vinegar/alum compress to your temples to help stop the bleeding. Dip a washcloth in a mixture of 1 pint vinegar and 1 ounce alum, and hold cloth to temples.

Vaginal itching

Gain relief from the itching of a vaginal yeast infection by drawing a bathtub of warm water and adding ½ cup salt and ½ cup vinegar. Sit in tub for at least 20 minutes. See a physician if itching remains after a week.

Combine 1 quart warm water, 2 tablespoons apple cider vinegar, and 1 to 2 teaspoons garlic oil. Then use mixture as a douche to control general vaginal itching. If itching persists for several days, see a doctor.

Taken With a Grain of Salt

At one time or another, the following have been recommended home treatments for some common conditions and ailments. Many are considered folk remedies and are not endorsed by doctors, but you never know—they may still be worth a try!

Baldness

Folk remedies for baldness have included regular bathing with salt water, eating parsnips daily, rub bing bald spot with onion, and drinking sage tea or rum in large quantities.

Bruises

Soak a thick slice of onion in vinegar, and apply onion slice to a bruise. Folk tradition claims this will advance the healing process.

Healthy living

Add 1 teaspoon apple cider vinegar and a little honey to an 8-ounce glass of water. Drink this daily to keep yourself feeling healthy.

Hiccups

One teaspoon to 1 tablespoon vinegar added to a glass of warm water and sipped slowly may get rid of hiccups.

Yeast Infections

The itchiness of a vaginal yeast infection can be relieved with a douche of warm water and vinegar. Add 2 tablespoons vinegar to 1 quart warm water, then douche, lying down and tilting pelvis upward to keep the liquid inside the body as long as possible. This mixture may be an effective treatment for preventing vaginal yeast infections; however, do not use it more than once a week. Too-frequent douching will destroy the naturally occurring, beneficial organisms that generally control vaginal infections in women. Also, do not use this solution if there is persistent redness or irritation. Be sure to see a doctor if symptoms persist and for any other vaginal infections.

Indigestion

Sipping apple cider vinegar after a heavy meal may aid in digestion. Mix 1 tablespoon honey and ¼ cup apple cider vinegar into a coffee mug, and fill with boiling water. Drink this before, during, or after a meal to aid digestion.

Insomnia

Mix 1 cup honey and 2 tablespoons vinegar, and store in an airtight container. Take 2 teaspoons of this if you're having trouble falling asleep.

Another nighttime sleep aid is a coffee mug of 1 tablespoon honey, ¼ cup apple cider vinegar, and enough hot water to fill. Drink this just before going to bed to help you sleep.

Leg cramps

Some say that drinking a glass of water with 1 tablespoon vinegar added will help control painful leg cramps in the middle of the night.

Morning sickness

Add 1 teaspoon apple cider vinegar to a glass of water in the morning to help control morning sickness.

Varicose veins

Relieve painful or swollen varicose veins by splashing them with vinegar.

Chapter 7

Fun With Salt and Vinegar

Salt and vinegar are inexpensive ingredients for dozens of fun-filled arts and crafts projects for children and adults. What's more, vinegar's chemical properties make it an interesting medium for demonstrating some scientific principles, and salt can perform tricks that people have been studying for hundreds of years. The ideas presented here are only a handful of the many exciting activities that are possible with salt and vinegar. *Please note:* Some of the projects for children require adult supervision.

Draw out the Artist in You!

Salt Dough

One of the most common creative uses for salt is to make a dough that is similar to molding clay and some of the popular play clays. Best of all, Salt Dough is easy to make and economical! Give this recipe a try with your children on the next rainy day or during school break.

1 cup salt
4 cups all-purpose flour
Medium-size bowl
1½ cups warm water
Rolling pin
*2 tablespoons vegetable oil**

Mix flour and salt together in bowl. Add water, then knead dough and roll out as you would cookie dough. Add a little bit of flour if dough gets too sticky to work with.

*Add vegetable oil to dough only if you intend to store it for use at a later time.

Vinegar Vignette

Old-time remedies for nosebleeds included inhaling straight vinegar through the nose or burning a vinegar-soaked rag and inhaling the smoke.

Salt Painting

This cool art project will take your children a couple of days to complete, but the results will be well worth the wait!

Clear self-adhesive vinyl
Scissors
Salt
Watercolors
Paintbrush
Construction paper
Glue
Coloring book (optional)

Cut self-adhesive vinyl into a size suitable for drawing a picture (8×10 inches is a good size). Peel backing from vinyl, then sprinkle entire sticky side with salt. Hold up vinyl, and gently shake off any excess salt. Let sit for 2 days.

Place sheet of vinyl, salty side up, on top of a coloring book picture to trace or over a plain piece of paper to make an original drawing. Using a set of watercolors and a paintbrush, paint salty side of vinyl to make the drawing. (If you're tracing a coloring book picture, be sure to stay within the lines!) Paint lightly; rubbing too hard could ruin the paintbrush. Let dry, then remove paper from underneath sheet of vinyl. Glue painted salt paper to a background piece of paper to make it sturdy. You can glue it either salty- or smooth-side up.

Sand Art With Salt

Sand art is a unique, 3-dimensional way to add color to drawings. Best of all, you can create these masterpieces with just table salt and food coloring. Have your kids give it a try!

½ cup salt for each color of "sand"
Resealable plastic sandwich bags
Food coloring
Old newspapers
White glue
Water
Plastic cup
Construction paper
Pencil
Large cookie sheet
Small paintbrush

First make colored sand by pouring ½ cup salt into a sandwich bag and adding several drops of food coloring. Close bag, making sure you squeeze all the air out before sealing. Use your fingers to massage coloring into salt. If it's not quite the right color, add more food coloring and massage again. When all the color is thoroughly mixed into salt, spread it onto a layer of newspaper, and let dry. Repeat steps for each color of sand you want. When all salt is dried out, carefully pour each color back into its sandwich bag.

Next mix white glue with an equal amount of water in a plastic cup. Use a pencil to draw a scene or design onto construction paper. Then place the piece of paper on a cookie sheet. Dip paintbrush into glue mixture, and paint over parts of your design you want to be all the same color. For example, if you have yellow sand and you want a sunflower in the scene to be all yellow, paint only the sunflower with the glue mixture.

After painting with your mixture, sprinkle desired color of sand over glued area. Wait a few minutes for the salt to stick to the glue, then gently lift and shake the construction paper over the cookie sheet to remove any loose salt. Pour any extra salt back into its original plastic sandwich bag to be used again. Repeat steps until your entire picture has been painted in various colors of salt.

Grain of Salt Department

Vinegar may help curb your appetite. Add 1 tablespoon vinegar and 1 tablespoon honey to an 8-ounce glass of water before a meal and you may not want to eat as much as usual. You can also combine 1 tablespoon apple cider vinegar and 1 tablespoon honey in an 8-ounce glass of unsweetened grapefruit juice. Drink 1 glass before each meal as an appetite suppressant.

How Crafty!

Applehead Doll

The dehydrating effect of salt can turn apples into interesting doll features. It will take several weeks to dry out the apples, however, so this project requires lots of patience!

½ gallon water
½ cup salt
½ cup lemon juice
Bucket or large bowl
1 firm red or green apple
Paring knife
18-gauge mechanic's wire
Needlenose pliers
2 black beads or buttons
Scrap fabric
Fiberfill
Yarn
Scissors
Needle
Thread
Wool or synthetic doll hair
Glue gun

Mix water, salt, and lemon juice in a bucket or large bowl. Peel apple, then soak it in water solution for 5 minutes. Using a paring knife, carve a face into apple. Make 2 slits for eyes and a U shape for a nose. (You may need an adult to help you with this.) Return carved apple to water solution. Remove apple after 10 minutes, and string a piece of wire through it from top to bottom. Hang apple to dry away from direct sunlight. After 1 week, insert black buttons into carved apple's eye slits. Apple will close in around buttons as it continues to dry. In about 2 weeks, apple will become leathery and pliable.

To assemble doll, cut wire into two 8-inch pieces and one 2-inch piece. Form an X with the two 8-inch sections, leaving wire at the top of the X (the arms) about 3 inches long. Wire at the bottom (the legs) will be about 5 inches long. Add 2-inch wire piece to the top of the X to form doll's neck. Pad the body by surrounding it first with scrap fabric then

Centerpieces

When making a centerpiece out of helium balloons, you can make a weight to coordinate with the theme. Fill an uninflated balloon with salt, using a funnel. Next wrap the filled balloon with tissue paper, and tie paper with ribbon. Tie helium balloon or balloons to this weighted balloon, and add any other decorations.

Use salt to hold artificial flowers in a vase or container while you are arranging them. Just pour in salt, add a little cold water, and arrange. As salt dries out, it will solidify around stems and create a stable base.

with fiberfill. Secure by wrapping yarn in a figure eight pattern around fiberfill. Follow these steps to also pad arms and legs. Then use scrap fabric to make clothes for the doll, or find appropriate-size doll clothing.

Secure head onto neck wire, then use a glue gun to affix hair to the head. Finish dressing and adding accessories to the doll, then pose as desired.

Gift Bath Salts

Save money on gifts by making your own fragrant bath salts. This is a great activity to do with your kids, too!

Large glass or metal mixing bowl
2 cups Epsom salt
1 cup sea salt, rock salt, or coarse salt
Food coloring
Metal spoon
¼ teaspoon glycerin
Essential oil for fragrance such as vanilla, citrus, or peppermint (optional)
Glass jars with screw-on metal lids or cork stoppers or clear gift bags

This project is best done on a day with low humidity, as the salt will absorb moisture in the air.

Combine salts in bowl, and mix well. Add food coloring, and stir with a metal spoon until well blended. (Food coloring will stain plastic or wooden spoons.) Add glycerin and about 4 to 5 drops of essential oil; stir again. Adjust coloring if desired by adding more food coloring.

Spoon colored salts into decorative glass jars or gift bags. Add a gift tag with instructions to use ⅓ to ½ cup of the salts in a bath.

Holiday Hoopla

A Tisket, a Tasket, a Salt Dough Bread Basket

This is a great activity for older children, and the end result can make a wonderful gift or holiday centerpiece.

7-inch glass bowl
Nonstick vegetable oil spray
Aluminum foil
Flour
Knife
Ruler
Pastry brush
Water
Cookie sheet
1 egg
Small bowl
Clear shellac or varnish

Salt Dough Ornaments

Use cookie cutters to cut Salt Dough (see page 86) into shapes for ornaments. After making shapes, punch a hole at the top of each shape to use for hanging. Place cutout pieces on a baking sheet, and bake at 250°F for 1 hour or until ornaments are dried out. Let ornaments cool, then decorate them using watercolors, tempera paint, or good-quality markers. You can experiment with glitter glue and fabric paints, too. When your design is ready, coat ornament with a clear protective coating, such as clear nail polish or varnish. When dry, thread decorative yarn or ribbon through hole or use a wire ornament hanger.

First make Salt Dough (see page 86). Set dough aside. Turn glass bowl upside down, and spray entire outside surface with nonstick spray. Then cover sprayed areas with aluminum foil. Smooth foil, and tuck extra edges inside bowl.

Salt Snippet

In 1863, during the Civil War, Union forces of the North cut the South off from its salt deposits on the Gulf Coast of Louisiana and destroyed important salt works in Florida, North Carolina, and Virginia.

Lightly flour a tabletop or breadboard, then roll salt dough into a rectangle shape at least 14 inches long and about ⅛ inch thick. Next cut strips 8¾ inches wide by 14 inches long. Lay out 4 strips of dough horizontally on your work surface. Weave remaining 4 strips vertically over and under first 4 strips, working very carefully. Don't leave any spaces between strips.

Using a pastry brush, spread water over the points where dough strips overlap. This will help bind them together. Slide woven strip section to edge of your tabletop, and hold bowl at counter level. Carefully slide strips onto bottom of the bowl. Overlap strips around edges of bowl and over each other. Press down in areas where strips bunch up.

Next cut remaining dough into 3 strips, each ¾ inch wide by 26 inches long. Roll each strip into a rope shape. When you've created 3 ropes, braid them together into 1 rope. Place braided rope around rim of bowl on top of woven strips. Overlap ½ inch where the 2 ends of the braid meet, and press these overlapped parts together. Trim off any excess dough. Moisten braided rope and lattice dough strips where they overlap, and gently press them together a little more. Place dough-covered bowl on a cookie sheet, and bake at 325°F for 30 minutes.

Take out of oven, and carefully remove dough from glass bowl. Keeping it upside down, place dough basket back onto cookie sheet. Beat 1 egg with 1 teaspoon water in a small bowl, then brush egg mixture onto dough basket. Return to oven and bake another 15 minutes or until basket is dry and golden brown. Remove to a wire cooling rack, and cool completely. Then shellac or varnish basket inside and out. Let dry 24 hours.

When Salt Dough Basket is complete, fill it with your favorite holiday decor, such as gourds, pumpkins, Christmas ornaments, pomanders, or any holiday-themed items.

Vinegar Vignette

A "vinaigrette" was originally a small, metal container used to carry a piece of sponge soaked in vinegar and combined with lavendar. These decorative boxes were used to hide the sponge while gentle folk inhaled the pleasant smell to mask the odor of their cities.

A Sampling of Science

Make a Motorboat

This easy science project will be boatloads of fun for both you and your children. Be sure to supervise kids during this activity.

Baking soda
Several squares of toilet paper
1 clean 16-ounce plastic soda bottle
¼ cup white vinegar
Bathtub or wading pool full of water

Pour 3 tablespoons baking soda onto a toilet paper square, and fold square into a packet to hold baking soda. Stuff folded toilet paper into soda bottle. You can add 1 or 2 more squares to bottle, but don't overstuff. Have bottlecap in 1 hand as you pour ¼ cup vinegar into bottle. Quickly put cap on, and twist once. Put bottle into bathtub or pool. The reaction between the baking soda and the vinegar should cause the bottle to "sail" across the water.

Vinegar Vignette

In 1864, the first fish-and-chips shops appeared in Britain when steam trawlers began shipping fish packed in ice. The fish were kept chilled until reaching the city, then they were deep fried along with potatoes. The only way to eat them was liberally doused in vinegar.

Create Your Own Fossils

You may not be able to find fossils in your backyard, but you can make your own with this super science project.

Mixing bowl
½ cup cold coffee
1 cup used coffee grounds
1 cup flour
½ cup salt
Waxed paper
Empty can or butter knife
Small objects like beads, coins, jewelry pieces, or shells
String (optional)

To make plaster, stir cold coffee and coffee grounds together in a bowl. Add flour and salt, and mix well to form a dough. Knead dough, then flatten onto a sheet of waxed paper. Use empty can to cut a circle in dough, or cut a square or rectangle out of dough with a butter knife. Cutouts should be large enough to hold the objects you are going to use to make a fossil impression.

Make patterns or indentations in plaster by firmly pressing small objects into dough. Be sure not to press too hard, or your object will poke through the back of the plaster shape. If you're going to hang your creation, poke a hole in the top of your dough so that when it hardens you'll be able to thread string through it. Let dough dry overnight, then hang the fossil.

Grow a Crystal Garden

Who said a garden was only made of flowers? This cool project is a sparkling alternative, and it's educational, too!

6 tablespoons salt
6 tablespoons liquid bluing (a laundry whitening product)
6 tablespoons water
1 tablespoon ammonia
Medium-size bowl
Small rocks or rock pieces
Shallow bowl
Food coloring
Tray or breadboard (optional)

Mix salt, bluing, water, and ammonia in a medium-size bowl. Place rocks in a shallow bowl. Pour mixture over rocks, then drip food coloring on top of rocks. Crystals will grow in about 3 weeks. After that time, keep adding water and they'll continue to grow. Place bowl on a tray or breadboard if crystals begin to grow over edges of bowl.

Why Salt the Water?

This experiment will show the effect salt has on boiling water. Many recipes require salted water, so here's your chance to figure out why.

Distilled water
2-quart cooking pot

Candy or cooking thermometer
Paper
Pen
Table salt

Boil 1 quart distilled water in a cooking pot on the stove. Use thermometer to measure temperature of boiling water. Record water temperature on a piece of paper. Add 1 teaspoon salt to boiling water, and stir. Measure water temperature again, and record on your paper. Add larger quantities of salt to water after it boils again, and take temperature reading each time. You should start to notice that adding salt to water raises the temperature at which it boils.

> **Vinegar Vignette**
>
> **It's a good idea to occasionally soak the mouthpiece of a saxophone in vinegar overnight to remove saliva stains.**

Clean Dirty Pennies

Shine up your pennies, and learn a thing or two about the chemical reaction between vinegar and copper.

¼ cup vinegar
1 teaspoon salt
Clear, shallow bowl (not metal)
20 very dirty pennies
Paper towels
2 rusty nails

Add vinegar and salt to bowl, and stir until salt dissolves. Using your fingers, dip 1 penny halfway into mixture, and hold it there for 10 seconds. What happened? The pennies should become shiny. The vinegar removes copper oxide, which is what causes pennies to become dirty-looking.

Next put remaining pennies into vinegar mixture. Watch them for a few seconds to see what happens. After 5 minutes, take 10 of the pennies out of the mixture and leave the others in. Put the ones you took out onto a paper towel to dry. Then remove the rest of the pennies, and rinse them under running water; place on a paper towel to dry. Are there differences in the 2 batches of pennies? You should observe that the unrinsed pennies turned blue-green. Now put 2 rusty nails into the vinegar mixture. Make sure one is

Analyze Acidic Reactions

Save a chicken bone from your next chicken dinner, and put it in a clear jar. Fill jar with vinegar, put lid on, and let sit 1 week. Observe what happens to the bone. The bone should become flexible because the vinegar has caused the calcium, which makes bones hard, to dissolve.

Put an egg still in its shell into a jar of vinegar, and check it the next day. What has happened to it? The eggshell, which is made of calcium, should become soft or disintegrate completely.

completely covered in the mixture and the other is leaning against the side of the bowl, only halfway into the mixture. After 10 minutes, look at nails and note differences. One should be completely shiny, and the one dipped halfway should be half shiny and half dull.

Study Dehydration With Salt

Before we had freezers and refrigerators, salt was an important preservative and was one of a few ways to keep food from spoiling. This exercise demonstrates how salt extracts the liquid from apples.

Masking tape
8 disposable 12-ounce cups
Permanent marker
2 fresh apples
Paring knife
Food scale
1 large box baking soda
1 box Epsom salts
1 box table salt
Large mixing bowl
Paper and pencil

Put large strip of masking tape on each cup to make a label, then number cups from 1 to 8. Slice each apple into 4 parts to create 8 slices. Weigh one of the apple slices. Write "starting weight" on cup #1, and put slice into cup. Repeat weighing and recording process, giving each apple slice its own cup. Now you're going to add various amounts of salt and/or baking soda to each cup and label accordingly. (See chart below.) Make sure the ingredients completely cover the apple slices.

Cup	Ingredient	Label
#1	½ cup baking soda	baking soda only
#2	½ cup Epsom salts	Epsom salts only
#3	½ cup table salt	table salt only
#4	¼ cup Epsom salts and ¼ cup table salt	Epsom salts and table salt
#5	¼ cup table salt and ¼ cup baking soda	table salt and baking soda
#6	¼ cup baking soda and ¼ cup Epsom salts	baking soda and Epsom salts
#7	⅓ cup each of baking soda, Epsom salts, and table salt	baking soda, Epsom salts, and table salt
#8	nothing	nothing

Place labeled cups in a safe place out of direct sunlight for 1 week. Then take out each apple slice, and brush off as much of the salt mixtures as possible. Do not rinse apples. Weigh each slice again, and record the new weights on the cups. Now calculate the percentage differences in each starting and ending weight, and record that percentage change on each cup. What did you learn? Did the apple slices look a lot different when you started this experiment? Which mixture caused the most loss of weight? The salt should take all the moisture out of some of the apple slices, depending on the amount of salt and other additives.

Lava Lamp Lesson

This project will demonstrate the properties of oil and water and show how lava lamps work.

Glass jar or clear drinking glass
Water
⅓ *cup vegetable oil*
Food coloring
Salt

Pour about 3 inches water into clear jar or glass. Add vegetable oil and 1 drop of food coloring to jar. Then shake salt on top of oil very slowly, counting to 5. Observe what happens to food coloring and salt. Add more salt to move oil blobs around again.

Make Magic Beans

Fill a clear vase with water, and add a little food coloring. Then add ¼ cup vinegar and 3 teaspoons baking soda. Drop in dried beans, buttons, pasta, or rice, and see what they do in the mixture. The small objects should rise to the top, then drop, then rise.

Chapter 8

The Great Outdoors

We've already seen hundreds of uses for salt and vinegar inside your home. Now learn about the many ways to use these wonderful ingredients outside, too! Salt and vinegar are great alternatives to toxic chemicals for controlling weeds, pests, and disease in your yard. For example, vinegar (particularly apple cider vinegar) is a key ingredient in organic herbicides and fertilizers, and salt is great at killing some pests. Beyond the garden, salt is an excellent deicer for winter climates, and both ingredients can work wonders with outdoor maintenance projects.

Great Gardening

Containers

Remove stains that develop in clay flowerpots by filling them with ⅔ cold water and ⅓ vinegar. Let pots soak until they look clean, then wash with soap and water, and rinse.

Preserving Roses

Treat fresh-cut roses with extra care by displaying them in sterile vases with a preservative. Instead of a commercial preservative, mix 1 gallon water, 1 tablespoon vinegar, and 1 tablespoon granulated sugar. Flowers in a preservative solution will last about twice as long as those in plain water. You can also extend the lives of your flowers by replacing the water in the container every 2 to 3 days.

Cut flowers

A simple preservative for a vase of cut flowers is 1 quart warm water to which you've added 2 tablespoons vinegar and 1 teaspoon sugar.

Use this simple mixture to extend the life of your cut flowers: Mix 1 quart water, 1 tablespoon sugar, 1 teaspoon vinegar, and 1 teaspoon mouthwash.

Plants

A squirt of vinegar may help invigorate a plant and make it more resistant to disease and pests.

Mix 1 ounce vinegar with 1 gallon compost tea, and use as a regular spray on garden plants.

Basic Organic Spray

Feed your foliage well with this homemade fertilizing spray.

Mix 1 ounce molasses, 1 cup manure-base compost tea,* 1 ounce liquid seaweed, and 1 ounce apple cider vinegar (natural is preferred) into a gallon of water. Add this liquid to a garden sprayer, and use on green plants in your garden.

***Making Compost Tea**

A compost tea is a way to use composting materials from your backyard as a concentrated fertilizer. To make the tea, place composted materials in a burlap bag, secure bag, and put it in a bucket of water. Use 1 part compost to 5 parts water. Let bag steep in water for 10 to 14 days, then remove and squeeze sack until it stops dripping. Discard sack, and save liquid as your tea.

Poison ivy

A strong solution of saltwater can kill an area infested with poison ivy plants. Mix 3 pounds salt with a gallon of soapy water. Apply to leaves and stems of poison ivy plants using a garden sprayer.

Roses

Mix 3 tablespoons natural apple cider vinegar in 1 gallon water. Fill garden sprayer with mixture, and spray roses daily to control black spot or other fungal diseases.

Organic Herbicide

Combat plant diseases by combining 1 gallon vinegar, 1 cup orange oil, and 1 teaspoon Basic H or other mild soap. Spray solution on plants with your garden sprayer.

Seedlings

If seedlings begin to mold while starting them in a damp medium, clean them with a solution of 1 part vinegar to 9 parts water, and transfer to a new container. Spritz seeds regularly with this diluted mixture while awaiting germination.

Reuse containers you may have from last season's nursery flats for seedling plants. Be sure to protect against plant disease by thoroughly cleaning containers in hot, soapy water. Then rinse using undiluted vinegar, which will help kill any lingering bacteria that could lead to disease.

Weeds

Boil 1 quart water, then add 2 tablespoons salt and 5 tablespoons vinegar to it. While still hot, pour mixture directly onto weeds between cracks on sidewalks and driveways.

Fill a spray bottle with undiluted vinegar, and apply directly onto weeds or unwanted grass. You may have to repeat, but you should see weeds gradually wilt away.

Start Your Seeds

You can improve the germination of some vegetable seeds such as okra and asparagus, which are woody and often difficult to start, by rubbing them with coarse sandpaper before planting. Rub seeds between 2 pieces of sandpaper, then soak seeds overnight in a pint of warm water to which you've added ½ cup vinegar and a squirt of liquid dish soap. Plant seeds as normal. Use this same method without the sandpaper rub for seeds like nasturtium, parsley, beets, and parsnips.

Pest Patrol

Ants

You may be able to stop a troop of ants from marching into your house if you can identify their points of entry and wipe areas with undiluted vinegar. Spray vinegar on thresholds, near sinks, or near appliances where ants are gathering.

Ordinary table salt sprinkled in areas where ants congregate may help deter them.

Cabbage worms

Cabbage worms frequently attack garden cabbages, broccoli, and cauliflower. To control them, dust the leaves of these vegetables with a mixture of 1 cup flour and ½ cup salt. Use this dusting powder in the morning or evening when plants are damp with dew.

Cats

Cats can wreak havoc on your garden by using it as a litter box. Soak wads of newspaper with vinegar, and scatter them in areas where cats have been. The vinegar smell should discourage repeat visits.

Cockroaches

A squirt of pure vinegar from a spray bottle may stop a cockroach long enough to be captured and disposed of properly.

Moths

Salt sprinkled directly on a moth will kill it.

Slugs

Slugs like to feed on gardens primarily at night or on cloudy, damp days. To combat them, fill a spray bottle with half vinegar and half water. Search out slugs at night, and kill them by squirting them directly with solution.

You can also kill slugs by sprinkling them with a heavy dose of salt. Wait 5 minutes, then sprinkle them again.

Camping Gear

Canvas

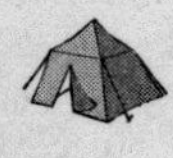
Deodorize canvas bags or any bags that have developed a musty smell by sprinkling the inside with salt, zipping up the bag, and letting it sit overnight. Remove salt in the morning, and allow bag to air out.

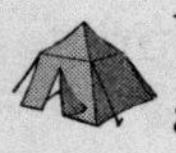
Use the Multipurpose Home Cleaner (see page 16) and a bristle scrub brush to clean canvas tents or other canvas materials. Dip brush in warm water, then spray on cleaner and brush.

If your tent develops mildew, clean problem areas by wiping them with vinegar and letting tent dry in the sun.

Coolers

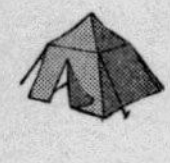
Picnic jugs and coolers often take on musty or mildewy smells. Rinse smelly items with undiluted vinegar, then wash with soap and water to clean thoroughly. Rinse.

Water kept in a closed container can taste stale. Keep your water supply fresh by adding a few drops of vinegar to bottle or canteen. The vinegar will also make the water a better thirst-quencher.

Fish

Rub a freshly caught fish with vinegar before cleaning and scaling it. The scaling will be easier, and the vinegar will help control the fishy odor on your hands.

Plastic

Plastic tarps or outdoor equipment coverings can be made antistatic by cleaning them with a solution of 1 tablespoon undiluted vinegar to 1 gallon water. This may also reduce the amount of dust attracted to the plastic covering.

Propane lanterns

Propane lantern casing can be made to last longer if it is first soaked in undiluted vinegar for several hours. Allow casing to dry, then light.

Rust

Clean the rust from bike handlebars or tire rims by making a paste of 6 tablespoons salt and

Salt Snippet

When you set out "to eat a man's salt," you will partake in his hospitality. Among Arabic people, to eat a man's salt created a sacred bond between the host and guest. No one who has eaten of another's salt should speak ill of him or treat him unkindly.

2 tablespoons lemon juice. Apply paste to rusted areas with a dry cloth, then rub, rinse, and dry thoroughly.

Vinegar Vignette

Throughout the world there are only 12 copies of something known as *The Vinegar Bible*, a version of the Christian Bible printed in 1717. The edition features beautiful engravings and elegant type. However, it also contains numerous typos, including a misuse of the word *vinegar*. In the New Testament's parable of the vineyard, the heading reads, "The parable of the vinegar."

Care for Your Car

Bugs

Remove dead bugs from the hood of your car with full-strength vinegar on a cloth.

Chrome

Shine chrome on any car using full-strength vinegar on a soft polishing cloth. The vinegar will not leave any spots behind.

Deodorizing

Perform an overnight deodorizing treatment on your car by soaking a piece of bread in vinegar and leaving it in the car overnight with the windows closed.

Oil spills

If you accidentally spill oil onto your garage floor, sprinkle salt on it and wait 15 minutes. The salt will help soak up some of the liquid and make cleaning up easier.

Salt stains

Get winter salt stains out of your car carpeting with a mixture of vinegar and water, scrubbed in and rinsed out thoroughly.

Stickers

Remove the price sticker sheet or other sticky-backed item from a car by soaking it with vinegar from a spray bottle, waiting a few minutes, then peeling off. Vinegar can also help remove any remaining glue residue.

Windshields

Avoid frosted car windows on a cold morning by rubbing them in the evening with a sponge dipped in a saltwater solution. Use 2 tablespoons salt to 2 cups water.

Fill a small cloth bag or folded scrap of cloth with salt, and hold securely closed. Dampen bag with water, then rub it on outside of windshield to keep snow and ice from adhering.

Another windshield treatment is a spray of 3 parts vinegar to 1 part water. Mix in a spray bottle, and spray windows in the evening. Frost will not develop on windows overnight.

More Outdoor Tips and Tricks

Patio furniture

If you've discovered your outdoor wicker furniture has mildewed while being stored for winter, remove mildew from affected areas by washing them with a mixture of vinegar and water. You can use undiluted vinegar for a really tough job. Use a stiff scrubbing brush to remove mildew in crevices. Dry furniture well with rags, then set it in the sun to dry completely.

Sidewalks

Rock salt is a mainstay for households in snowy climates. If spread on driveways or sidewalks before snow or sleet falls, it will keep ice crystals from bonding to the surface and keep it safe for walking.

Salt Snippet

In 1930, citizens of India began a campaign against their British occupiers and their monopoly on salt production. Civil disobedience leader Mahatma Gandhi led people to the Arabian Sea, and they produced salt by evaporating seawater, a violation of British-imposed law.

Chapter 9

Pet and Animal Care

You might be surprised to learn that vinegar is a horse's best friend (it controls flies) and that salt can combat a flea infestation in your home, perhaps as well as a toxic flea bomb. It never hurts to know exactly what you're feeding your pets, so this chapter also includes some recipes for homemade treats that use vinegar or salt. Your pets will thank you!

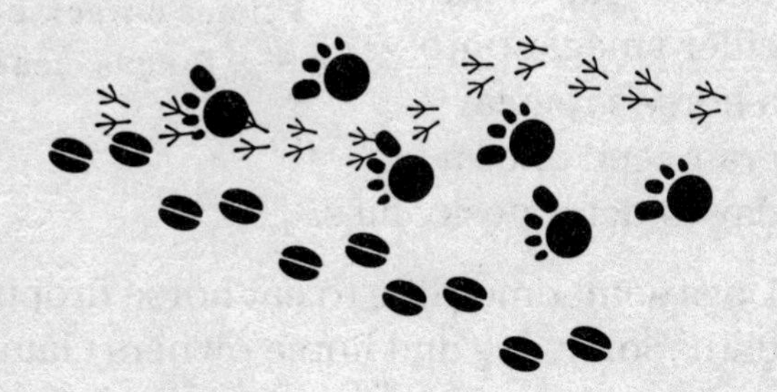

In the Barnyard

Chickens

Use white or apple cider vinegar to clean out a chicken's water container. Pour vinegar directly onto a rag and wipe containers, then rinse with water.

Horses

Spruce up a horse's coat by adding ½ cup vinegar to 1 quart water. Use this mixture in a spray bottle to apply to the horse's coat before showing.

Pour ¼ cup apple cider vinegar onto a horse's regular grain feed once a day to deter pesky flies.

Treat White Line Disease

Some horse owners claim that White Line Disease, a fungus that infiltrates a horse's hoof, can be treated with ½ cup white vinegar mixed with 8 cups water and 1 cup copper sulfate. The horse's hooves should be soaked in this solution for 15 minutes for each hoof. Do this at least 5 times a week until the fungus clears.

Dogs sometimes like to eat horse droppings in the barn. Some dog and horse owners claim that adding ½ cup vinegar to the horse's feed 2 times a day will discourage dogs from doing this.

Homemade Horse Treats

Feed homemade treats to your horse, and you'll know what he's getting. Here's a recipe that will make a large quantity of nibbles to keep on hand.

In large bowl, mix 1 cup molasses; ½ cup brown sugar; 4 large carrots, shredded; 1 cup finely chopped apples; and ½ cup apple cider vinegar. In another bowl, mix 2 cups bran, 1 cup sweet feed, and 1 cup flaxseed. Slowly add molasses mixture to dry ingredients until a dough forms. If dough is too thick, add more vinegar. If it becomes runny, add more bran. Drop batter onto a cookie sheet lined with aluminum foil, using a tablespoon. Flatten each piece of dough slightly, then bake at 300°F for 1 hour. Turn cookies over with a spatula, and continue baking until they are completely dried, about another 45 minutes. Allow cookies to cool before feeding. Store in an airtight container.

Household Pets

Cats

Use vinegar to clean out a kitty litter pan. Remove litter, and pour in ½ inch vinegar. Let vinegar stand 15 minutes. Pour out, and thoroughly dry the pan. Then sprinkle with baking soda, and add fresh kitty litter.

If you're trying to keep your cats from walking on, sleeping on, or scratching certain items in your home, lightly sprinkle items with vinegar. The smell will keep cats away.

Add 1 tablespoon apple cider vinegar to your cat or dog's water bowl to improve overall health and digestion.

Clean up urinary accidents from cats or dogs in your home by drying soiled area and then applying undiluted vinegar. The vinegar will help control odor and keep your pet from visiting the area again (see also Chapter 2).

Grain of Salt Department

Chickens: **Rumor has it that chickens who drink water laced with a little vinegar will not peck each other. Another theory states that vinegar in a chicken's water will keep her laying eggs better throughout the winter months and will maintain the chicken's health.**

Rabbits: **Rabbit raisers claim that vinegar added to water can help a female rabbit feel "in the mood" when it's time to breed with the male rabbit.**

Dogs

Minimize soap residue after a dog's shampoo by adding vinegar to rinse water. Rinse again with plain water.

Flea-Be-Gone Dog Treats

Frugal dog owners can make a batch of homemade biscuits as treats. They will keep for weeks, are cheaper than store-bought varieties, and can even help control fleas. A batch of these would make a great gift for any dog lover.

Stir 3 tablespoons vegetable oil and 1 tablespoon garlic powder together in a large mixing bowl. In another bowl, mix 2 cups flour, ½ cup wheat germ, ½ cup brewer's yeast, and 1 teaspoon salt. Slowly add oil and garlic mixture to dry ingredients, and stir in 1 cup chicken broth when mixture gets too dry. Mix thoroughly until you get a dough consistency. Roll dough onto a floured surface to about ¼ inch thick. Use knife to cut dough into squares, or, for a special treat, use cookie cutters to make dough shapes. Place shapes onto a large, greased baking sheet, and bake at 350°F for 20 to 25 minutes or until edges are brown. Allow to cool 2 hours, then store in plastic bags in a location dogs can't reach.

Using vinegar as an after-shampoo treatment can make a dog's itchy skin feel better and his coat look shinier. Mix ½ cup vinegar into 1 gallon water, and coat dog's hair with solution. Leave it on coat for 10 minutes, then rinse thoroughly. Be sure to keep shampoo out of dog's eyes during this treatment.

After a therapeutic shampoo to treat a skin infection, rinse dog with a solution of 1 part apple cider vinegar to 3 parts water.

Floppy-eared dogs can be prone to yeast infections in their ears, especially after bathing or grooming. To avoid getting water in your dog's ears, plug ears with cotton balls moistened with apple cider vinegar.

Care for Ears

Create a solution of ⅓ vinegar, ⅓ rubbing alcohol, and ⅓ water. For dogs and cats, use an eyedropper to put about 8 to 10 drops in each ear once a month to facilitate cleaning. Let solution sit in ear 1 minute, then tilt pet's head to drain. Wipe away excess liquid. This solution may also prevent ear infections. If persistent scratching or other signs of trouble persist, see a vet. Excessive itching may mean mites or a bacterial infection.

Control general scratching by regularly wiping your dog or cat's ear area with a cloth dipped in vinegar.

Another ear-cleaning remedy is to mix 1 tablespoon vinegar, 1 tablespoon hydrogen peroxide, 1 table-

Fiber for Fido

The bran in this doggie treat recipe will provide your pet with much needed fiber.

In a very large mixing bowl, combine 2 tablespoons wheat germ, ¼ cup crushed bran flakes, 1 cup whole wheat flour, ⅛ cup corn meal, ⅛ cup white flour, 1 tablespoon molasses, 2 tablespoons vegetable shortening, 1 teaspoon sage, 1 bouillon cube dissolved in ⅓ cup warm water, and 1 teaspoon salt.

Pour small batches of mixture into food processor and blend, adding water as mixture balls up. When it becomes 1 ball of dough, flatten and roll it onto a breadboard. Cut shapes out of dough with a cookie cutter or knife. Lightly grease a cookie sheet, and bake treats for 30 minutes at 350°F. Cool, and store in an airtight container.

spoon yucca root tea (available at heath food stores), 1 drop lavender oil, and ½ cup aloe vera gel. Apply to dog or cat's ear with cotton swabs to clean.

If you've had a flea infestation in your home, sprinkle carpet or rugs with salt to help kill any flea eggs. Let stand a few hours, then vacuum. Repeat weekly for 6 weeks.

Fish Snacks

Some pet fish like to eat the eggs of brine shrimp, but they prefer these eggs to be deshelled. To remove shells from a tablespoon of shrimp eggs, soak eggs for 15 minutes in an inch of water in a jar. Then add an equal amount of bleach to water; stir. When eggs change color from brown to orange, pour them into a shrimp net, and rinse them with water. Fill jar again with water to about ¾ full, and add ¼ inch vinegar. Pour this vinegar water onto the eggs in the net, making sure they all get saturated. Now rinse thoroughly with fresh water, and feed them to your fish.

Something else to feed your fish: vinegar eels! The vinegar eel is a roundworm that likes to live in very acidic conditions—like vinegar. If you're interested in growing them to feed to your fish, just mix 1 part apple cider vinegar to 3 parts water, occasionally add a piece of apple, and your eel will be hatching in no time. They can live for a long time in an aquarium, are a great size for baby fish to eat, and require little attention.

Put salt in your vacuum cleaner bag to help kill flea eggs that may have been vacuumed up.

Relieve the odor of a dog who has had a tussle with a skunk by rinsing his coat with undiluted vinegar.

Be sure to keep vinegar out of the dog's eyes during this process. Some skunk smell may remain, but it will be kept under control as it gradually wears off.

If your dog comes home with a swollen nose, most likely he's been stung by a wasp. Make him feel better by bathing the affected area in vinegar.

Clean Stones for Aquariums

You can collect average stones from your backyard and use them in your aquariums, as long as you take some precautions so as not to introduce strange organisms into the water. Test your rocks first by pouring a small amount of vinegar onto their surfaces. If the vinegar fizzes at all, you won't want to use them in your aquarium because they will probably affect the water's pH balance and, therefore, affect the health of your fish.

Fish

Rub the inside glass of a fish tank with plain, non-iodized salt. Use a plastic pot scrubber to remove hard-water deposits or other buildup. Rinse well before returning fish to tank.

Give your goldfish a little swim in saltwater for a change of pace and to perk them up. Add 1 teaspoon salt to a quart of fresh water, and let fish swim for 15 minutes. Then return them to normal conditions.

Parrots

Some birdcages with hardware cloth (a type of wire) can lead to zinc poisoning, which is very harmful to parrots. Decrease the chance of poisoning by wiping entire cage with vinegar on a cloth before use.

Rabbits

Use vinegar to clean out rabbit litter boxes to control buildup of dried urine.

Vinegar Vignette

Some arachnid collectors take great pride in adding a Giant Vinegaroon, a member of the whip-scorpion family, to their collection. These 6-inch creatures look pretty nasty, but their main mode of defense is giving off a vinegar-scented acid from one of their glands. The acid won't generally harm people unless they are allergic to it, but a Vinegaroon's pinchers can do some damage. Some people keep them as pets, but you generally won't encounter one by chance because it hides by day and hunts at night. This creepy-looking arachnid is found only in the south and southwestern regions of the United States.

Chapter 10

Cooking Tips

When it comes to cooking, vinegar and salt have more jobs to do than just appearing as ingredients in recipes. They can perform miraculous tricks for improving flavor, preserving food, filling in for missing ingredients, and even making food look better. These ingredients can prevent spoilage and salvage some inevitable cooking disasters. In fact, if you add a pinch here and a drop there during the preparation process, vinegar and salt may change the whole personality of certain foods.

Cooking Tricks

Condiments

When getting to the bottom of a catsup bottle, add a little vinegar, and swish it around to make catsup stretch further. This technique will work for other condiments as well.

Dairy products

You can still hard-boil a cracked egg by adding 1 tablespoon vinegar to the boiling water. The vinegar will prevent egg white from running out.

Add a pinch of salt to any plain or mild-flavored yogurt to give it extra zing.

Fish and seafood

Add a tablespoon or more of vinegar to fried or boiled fish when cooking to reduce fishy tastes and smells and to keep meat soft.

Freshen up fish just brought home from the market by returning it to its natural environment for a short time. Add 1 tablespoon sea salt to 2 quarts cold water, then add a lot of ice cubes. Soak fish in this saltwater for about 15 minutes, then remove it and dry it off before preparing as desired.

Give canned shrimp and fish a freshly caught taste by covering it in sherry and adding 2 tablespoons vinegar. Soak for 15 minutes, then prepare as desired.

To keep fish white, soak it for 20 minutes in a mixture of 1 quart water and 2 tablespoons vinegar.

To get a good grip on a fish while trying to skin it for cooking, sprinkle your hands with salt.

Fruits and vegetables

When cooking fruit on the stovetop, add a spoonful of vinegar to improve flavor.

To poach asparagus, add salt to water, and simmer exactly 5 minutes. Stalks should all be pointing in the same direction. (Some culinary experts insist the asparagus sit upright in the boiling pot.)

When making mashed potatoes, add 1 tablespoon vinegar once you've used enough milk. This will help keep potatoes white. Whip them to desired consistency.

Get rid of the bitter juices in an eggplant by slicing eggplant and sprinkling slices with salt. Stand slices on end in a rack placed in a shallow pan, and let sit half an hour.

Use up the usually unusable portions of broccoli stalks by cutting them into 1-inch-thick slices. Stir fry them with salt, and eat as a snack.

After cutting hot chili peppers, be sure to scrub your hands and nails with soapy water. Then soak them in saltwater, and rinse. This will prevent getting stinging chili oil in your eyes.

In a tomato sauce or a tomato-base soup, add 1 or 2 tablespoons vinegar just before completing the cooking process. Flavors will be enhanced.

Meat

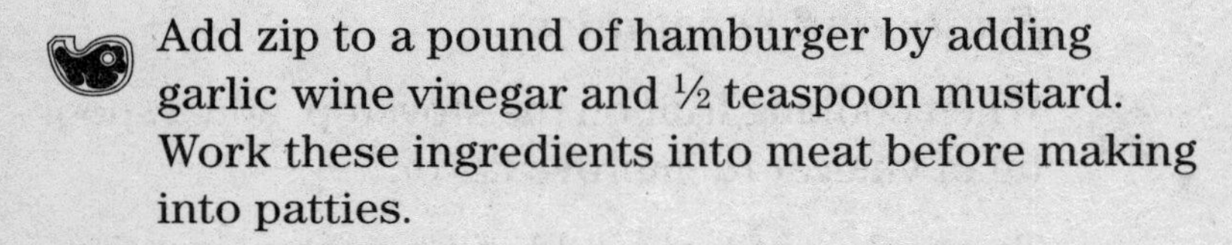

Add zip to a pound of hamburger by adding garlic wine vinegar and ½ teaspoon mustard. Work these ingredients into meat before making into patties.

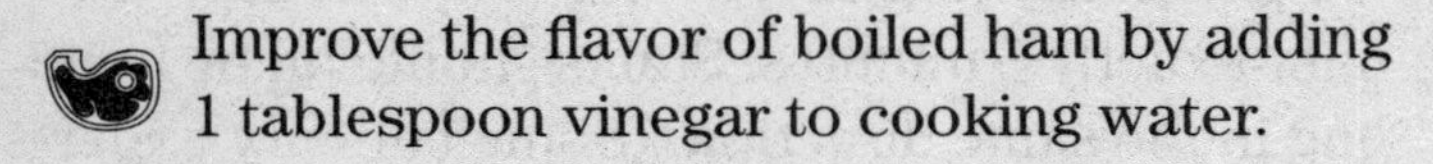

Improve the flavor of boiled ham by adding 1 tablespoon vinegar to cooking water.

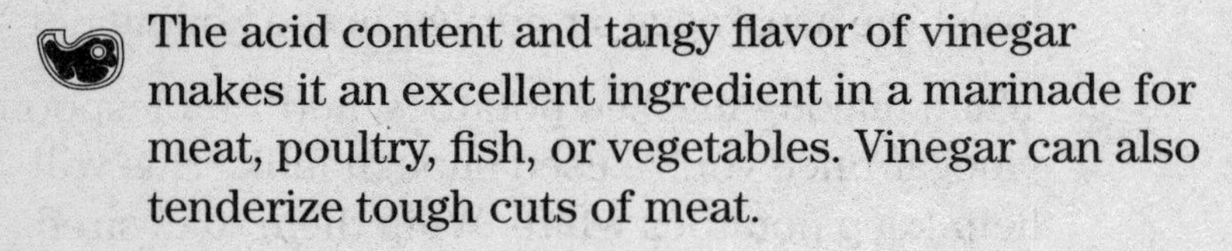

The acid content and tangy flavor of vinegar makes it an excellent ingredient in a marinade for meat, poultry, fish, or vegetables. Vinegar can also tenderize tough cuts of meat.

Salt will force juices out of meat and will prevent it from browning. Wait to salt meat until midway in the cooking process, then salt it lightly, or wait until cooking is complete, then salt to taste.

To make wild game taste less gamey, soak it before cooking in a vinegar/water solution. Use 1 part vinegar to 4 parts water to cover.

Pasta

Adding salt to pasta cooking water is a good idea, but wait until water boils. Then add 2 tablespoons salt for each pound of pasta. If you salt the water before it boils, it will take longer to boil.

Seasoning

- Salvage a dish to which you've added too much salt by adding a teaspoon of vinegar and sugar and then reheating.
- Sprinkle peeled garlic cloves with a little coarse salt before attempting to chop them. The salt will absorb garlic's juice and then dissolve, which will help spread garlic flavor further.
- Kosher salt can be kept in a pepper mill and twisted out as needed.

Herbal Salts

Create these herbal salts, and store them with your spices to use in soups and stews or vegetable, chicken, and fish dishes.

Chop a handful of fresh herb leaves, then add salt to them. Crush salt/herb mixture with a mortar and pestle, or put in a blender and chop for 5 to 10 minutes. Spread mixture onto a cookie sheet in a shallow layer. Heat oven to 200°F. Bake salt/herb mixture 40 to 60 minutes, stirring frequently to break up any lumps. Remove from oven, and cool on a cookie sheet. Store salts in a sealed jar away from heat and direct sunlight.

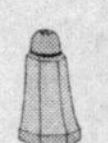

- If salt hardens at the bottom of your box of salt or saltshaker, use wooden chopsticks to loosen it.

- Since many recipes call for adding salt and pepper, prepare a premade mixture of both, and keep them in a separate shaker by your stove top. Use 3 parts salt to 1 part pepper.

Making Vinegar From Scratch

Apple cider vinegar

Plain apple cider can easily be made into apple cider vinegar if left to stand in an open bottle for about 5 weeks. The bottle should be kept at 70°F. It will first become hard cider and then vinegar.

Make instant apple cider vinegar by using plain apple cider. Just add brown sugar, molasses, or yeast, and watch it ferment.

Old-fashioned Apple Cider Vinegar

Cut up apples, and place them in a stone crock. Cover them with warm water, then tie a cheesecloth over the crock. Let sit in a warm place for 4 to 6 months. Strain off liquid, which by this time has become vinegar. To speed up fermentation process, add a lump of raw bread to crock. The yeast in the bread speeds up the natural fermentation process. After straining liquid, let it sit for 4 to 6 weeks before using as cider vinegar.

Chili vinegar

Put 3 ounces chopped chilies into 1 quart vinegar, and store for

2 weeks in a capped bottle. Strain liquid after 2 weeks. For a spicier, stronger vinegar, let chilies steep longer, to taste.

Cucumber-onion vinegar

Boil 1 pint vinegar, and add 1 teaspoon salt and a dash of white pepper. Add 2 sliced pickling cucumbers and 1 small onion, sliced very thin, to vinegar mixture. Store in a capped glass jar for 5 weeks, then strain. Pour strained liquid into a recycled wine bottle, and cork it. *Variation:* Leave out onion for a very light vinegar that's excellent on fruit salads.

Garlic vinegar

Peel cloves from 1 large bulb of garlic, and add them to 1 quart vinegar. Steep liquid for 2 weeks, then strain and discard garlic. Use a few drops for flavoring salads, cooked meat, or vegetables. *Variation:* Use 1 quart red wine vinegar for a resulting vinegar that can be used in place of fresh garlic in most recipes. One teaspoon of the garlic vinegar will be equivalent to a small clove of garlic.

Hot pepper vinegar

Pour 1 pint vinegar into a clean bottle with cap, then add ½ ounce cayenne pepper to it. Let mixture sit for 2 weeks out of direct sunlight. Shake bottle about every other day. After 2 weeks, strain and pour into a separate clean bottle for use.

Raspberry vinegar

Make a raspberry vinegar with 2 quarts water and 5 quarts red or black raspberries. Pour water over 1 quart washed red or black raspberries, and keep in airtight container. Let stand over-night, then strain and keep liquid (discard raspberries). Pour liquid over another quart of raspberries, then strain and discard raspberries. Add 1 pound sugar to strained liquid, and stir until dissolved. Let mixture stand uncovered for 2 months, strain, then use as vinegar.

Herbal Vinegars

Use homegrown herbs such as oregano, rosemary, tarragon, thyme, sage, or basil to make herbal vinegars. First sterilize decorative bottle by immersing it in a boiling water bath for 10 minutes (see page 146). Allow to cool. Wash fresh herbs thoroughly. Put 4 sprigs of herb into bottle, then fill bottle with vinegar. Seal and store in a cool, dark place for 2 weeks. The herb may decompose during the storage time. If so, remove it, and strain vinegar into a new bottle. Present your finished herbal vinegar as a gift in a decorative bottle.

Strawberry vinegar

Combine a bottle of white wine vinegar with ½ cup fresh, washed, and stemmed strawberries. Cover and let it sit at room temperature for 1 week. Remove fruit, and use vinegar in recipes calling for fruit vinegar, or sprinkle on a lettuce salad.

Tarragon vinegar

For a vinegar that's wonderful on cooked or raw vegetables, add ¼ cup tarragon leaves to a pint bottle of vinegar. Let stand, capped, for 8 weeks. Strain, and rebottle clean liquid.

White wine vinegar

Make a white wine vinegar at home by adding 2 pounds raisins to 1 gallon water. Let sit in a warm place for 2 months. Strain vinegar, then pour it into a decorative bottle. Make more vinegar by adding another ½ pound raisins to the dredges and going through the process again.

Baking Tips

Baking soda

Use vinegar to determine if old baking soda is still good enough for baking. Pour 2 tablespoons vinegar in a small dish, and add 1 teaspoon baking soda. Good baking soda should make the vinegar froth significantly.

Bread

Make the crust of homemade bread a nice, golden brown by removing it from the oven shortly before baking time is complete and brushing it with vinegar. Return to oven to finish baking.

You can help homemade bread rise by adding 1 tablespoon vinegar for every 2½ cups flour in the recipe. Reduce other liquids in recipe proportionately.

Meringue

Make a fluffier meringue that is also more stable by adding vinegar to batter before beating. For every 3 egg whites in recipe, add ½ teaspoon vinegar.

Pies

Reduce the overly sweet flavor in fruit pies or other desserts by adding a teaspoon of vinegar.

Food Preservation

Canning and pickling

After canning or pickling, the last step in the process should be to wipe outside of canning jars with undiluted vinegar on a sponge. This should prevent development of mold while cans are in storage.

Cheese

Wrap leftover hard cheese in a cloth saturated with vinegar, then store in an airtight container. This

Preserving Herbs

Preserve your homegrown herbs by making them into flavorful vinegar. Add herb leaves or seeds to white vinegar or apple cider vinegar. Cider vinegar is recommended for some of the stronger herbs such as dill, garlic, garlic chives, and horseradish. Balsamic vinegar or vinegar made with sherry or champagne is best for preserving oregano. Use ½ cup to 1 cup freshly crushed or bruised herb leaves to every 2 cups vinegar. The vinegar must completely cover the leaves. Store mixture in a sealed, nonmetal container (metal will react with the vinegar), and let it sit in a cool, dark place. Sample vinegar after a week to see if the flavor is as you would like. After 4 weeks, you will have extracted all the possible flavor out of the herb. Pour vinegar into decorative bottles with caps or cork stoppers. Unopened, the flavored vinegar will last up to 2 years. Opened, it will last 3 to 6 months.

You can also preserve herbs with salt. Just spread a thin layer of kosher salt in an airtight, rectangular container. Layer fresh herbs over salt (works best with basil, sage, or mint). Spread another thin layer of salt over herbs, then repeat layering process. Cover and store with your spices. To use, remove salt to expose herbs. Some may be darkened, but their flavor will be fine.

will keep cheese from molding or becoming hard.

Fruits and vegetables

If you have vegetables like spinach or lettuce that have wilted a bit, freshen them by soaking them in 2 cups water and 1 tablespoon vinegar.

Steamed vegetables will retain their color if 2 tablespoons vinegar are added to the water as vegetables steam.

Keep cauliflower white when boiling by adding a spoonful of vinegar to boiling water.

Make your own acidulated water, which is used to prevent fruits and vegetables from discoloring while you prepare them, by mixing ½ cup white vinegar and 2 quarts water. Soak cut vegetables or fruit in this mixture until ready to prepare or serve.

Toss chopped potatoes, apples, or avocados with 1 or 2 teaspoons vinegar to keep them from turning brown during cooking preparation. You can also add vinegar to a bowl of water in which you are temporarily storing these peeled items.

Ham

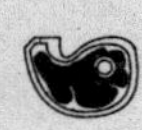

To keep mold from developing on a piece of uncooked ham stored in the refrigerator, rub vinegar onto cut end of the ham.

Recipe Substitutes

> ### Frozen Eggs
> **You can freeze eggs to preserve them, but you have to take them out of their shells first. Save yokes and whites, or just whites, by adding ⅛ teaspoon of salt to every ¼ cup of egg. Make sure you label the freezer container to reflect the date and that salt has been added so it won't affect a future recipe.**

Buttermilk

As a substitute for buttermilk, stir 1 tablespoon vinegar into 1 cup whole milk, and let stand a few minutes. Then measure out the amount called for in the recipe.

Lemons and limes

Vinegar can be used in any recipe calling for lemon or lime juice. Use ½ teaspoon vinegar for each teaspoon of lemon or lime.

Salt

If you're trying to cut back on salt in your diet, use vinegar as a seasoning for foods such as potatoes or other vegetables. Just sprinkle on lightly. Experiment with flavored, balsamic, wine, or rice vinegars.

Wine

You can substitute vinegar for wine in any recipe if you mix it with water first. Mix a ratio of 1 part vinegar to 3 parts water, then use whatever amount your recipe called for in place of the wine.

Flavorful Balsamic Vinegar

Balsamic vinegar, which has a robust flavor already, can make a great salt substitute for flavoring vegetables, fish, meat, or poultry. For additional flavor, add a large pinch of brown sugar per tablespoon of vinegar.

Food Cleaners

Fruits and vegetables

To remove dirt and pesticide residue from fresh fruits and vegetables, rinse them with 1 tablespoon vinegar added to 1 gallon warm water.

Salt can help remove the gritty dirt that comes with some fresh vegetables. When washing arugula, leeks, or spinach, trim them first, then place them in a bowl of lukewarm water. Add a tablespoon of kosher salt, swish, and let vegetables soak for 20 to 30 minutes. Transfer vegetables to a colander, and rinse thoroughly.

Chapter 11

Recipes

Can you imagine life without salt and vinegar? Many of our foods wouldn't be quite as flavorful, and some of them would spoil before you could even eat them! Salt shows up in so many recipes, often to draw out the flavor of certain ingredients, while vinegar can add zest to sauces, dressings, and much more. Read on for just a sampling of the dozens of recipes that rely on these two powerful ingredients.

Main Dishes

Sauerbraten

1 boneless beef sirloin tip roast (1¼ pounds)
3 cups baby carrots
1½ cups fresh or frozen pearl onions
¼ cup raisins
½ cup water
½ cup red wine vinegar
1 tablespoon honey
½ teaspoon salt
½ teaspoon dry mustard
½ teaspoon garlic-pepper seasoning
¼ teaspoon ground cloves
¼ cup crushed crisp gingersnap cookies (5 cookies)

Slow Cooker Directions

1. Heat large nonstick skillet over medium heat until hot. Brown roast on all sides; set aside.

2. Place roast, carrots, onions, and raisins in slow cooker. Combine water, vinegar, honey, salt, mustard, garlic-pepper seasoning, and cloves in large bowl; mix well. Pour mixture over meat and vegetables.

3. Cover and cook on low 4 to 6 hours or until internal temperature reaches 145°F when tested with meat thermometer inserted into thickest part of roast. Transfer roast to cutting board; cover with foil. Let stand 10 to 15 minutes before slicing. Internal temperature will continue to rise 5° to 10°F during stand time.

4. Remove vegetables with slotted spoon to bowl; cover to keep warm. Stir crushed cookies into sauce mixture in slow cooker. Cover and cook on high 10 to 15 minutes or until sauce thickens. Serve meat and vegetables with sauce.

Makes 5 servings

Roast Pork Chops With Apples and Cabbage

3 teaspoons olive oil, divided
½ medium onion, thinly sliced
1 teaspoon dried thyme leaves
2 cloves garlic, minced
4 pork chops, 1 inch thick (6 to 8 ounces each)
Salt and pepper, to taste
¼ cup cider vinegar
1 tablespoon packed brown sugar
¼ teaspoon black pepper
1 large McIntosh apple, chopped
½ (8-ounce) package preshredded coleslaw mix

1. Heat 2 teaspoons oil in large skillet over medium-high heat until hot. Add onion; cook, covered, 4 to 6 minutes or until onion is tender, stirring often. Add thyme and garlic; stir 30 seconds. Transfer to small bowl; set aside.

2. Add remaining 1 teaspoon oil to skillet. Sprinkle pork chops

Salt Snippet

To say a person is "not worth his salt" means he is not worth the expense of the food he eats.

with salt and pepper. Place in skillet; cook 2 minutes per side or until browned. Transfer pork chops to plate. Cover and refrigerate up to 1 day.

3. Remove skillet from heat. Add vinegar, sugar, and ¼ teaspoon pepper; stir to dissolve sugar and scrape cooked bits from skillet. Pour mixture into large bowl. Add onion mixture, apple, and coleslaw mix; do not stir. Cover and refrigerate up to 1 day.

4. To complete recipe, preheat oven to 375°F. Place cabbage mixture in large ovenproof skillet. Heat over medium-high heat; stir until blended and liquid comes to a boil. Lay pork chops on top of cabbage mixture, overlapping to fit. Cover pan; place in oven. Bake 15 minutes or until pork chops are juicy and just barely pink in center.

Makes 4 servings

Note: Instead of making ahead, prepare recipe through step 2 as directed above using ovenproof skillet, but do not refrigerate pork chops. Combine vinegar mixture,

Salt Snippet

Our word *salary*, the pay we receive from employers, originated during the Roman empire when soldiers and civil servants were paid with rations of salt and other necessities. Together any such rations were referred to as *salt*.

onion mixture, apple, and cabbage in skillet; bring to a boil and top with pork chops. Complete recipe as directed.

Jamaican Baby Back Ribs

2 tablespoons sugar
2 tablespoons fresh lemon juice
1 tablespoon salt
1 tablespoon vegetable oil
2 teaspoons black pepper
2 teaspoons dried thyme leaves, crushed
¾ teaspoon each ground cinnamon, nutmeg, and allspice
½ teaspoon ground red pepper
6 pounds well-trimmed pork baby back ribs, cut into 3- to 4-rib portions
Barbecue Sauce (recipe follows)

1. For seasoning rub, combine all ingredients except ribs and Barbecue Sauce in small bowl; stir well. Spread over all surfaces of ribs; press with fingertips so mixture adheres to ribs. Cover; refrigerate overnight.

2. Prepare grill for indirect cooking. While coals are heating, prepare Barbecue Sauce.

3. Baste ribs generously with Barbecue Sauce; grill 30 minutes more or until ribs are tender and browned, turning occasionally.

4. Bring remaining Barbecue Sauce to a boil over medium-high heat; boil 1 minute. Serve ribs with remaining sauce.

Makes 6 servings

Barbecue Sauce

2 tablespoons butter
½ cup finely chopped onion
1½ cups ketchup
1 cup red currant jelly
¼ cup apple cider vinegar
1 tablespoon soy sauce
¼ teaspoon each ground red and black peppers

Melt butter in medium saucepan over medium-high heat. Add onion; cook and stir until softened. Stir in remaining ingredients. Reduce heat to medium-low; simmer 20 minutes, stirring often.

Makes about 3 cups

Barbecued Ham

Soak thin slices of ham 1 hour in lukewarm water. Drain, wipe, and cook in a hot frying pan until slightly browned. Remove to serving dish. Add 3 tablespoons vinegar, 1½ teaspoons mustard, 1½ teaspoons sugar, and ⅛ teaspoon paprika to fat in pan. When thoroughly heated, pour mixture over ham and serve immediately.

Szechuan Grilled Flank Steak

1 beef flank steak (1¼ to 1½ pounds)
¼ cup soy sauce
¼ cup seasoned rice vinegar
2 tablespoons dark sesame oil
4 cloves garlic, minced
2 teaspoons fresh ginger, minced
½ teaspoon red pepper flakes
¼ cup water

½ cup green onions, thinly sliced
2 to 3 teaspoons sesame seeds, toasted
Hot cooked rice (optional)

1. Place steak in large resealable plastic food storage bag. To prepare marinade, combine soy sauce, vinegar, oil, garlic, ginger, and red pepper flakes in small bowl; pour over steak. Press air from bag and seal; turn to coat. Marinate in refrigerator 3 hours, turning once.

2. To prevent sticking, spray grid with nonstick cooking spray. Prepare coals for grilling. Drain steak, reserving marinade in small saucepan. Place steak on grid; grill, covered, over medium-hot coals 14 to 18 minutes for medium or to desired doneness, turning steak halfway through grilling time.

3. Add water to reserved marinade. Bring to a boil over high heat. Reduce heat to low; simmer 5 minutes. Transfer steak to carving board. Slice steak across grain into thin slices. Drizzle steak with boiled marinade. Sprinkle with green onions and sesame seeds. Serve with rice.

Makes 4 to 6 servings

Side Dishes

Marinated Whole Mushrooms

7 pounds small whole mushrooms
½ cup bottled lemon juice
2½ cups white vinegar (5 percent)

2 cups olive or salad oil
1 tablespoon canning or pickling salt
1 tablespoon dried oregano leaves
1 tablespoon dried basil leaves
½ cup finely chopped onions
¼ cup diced pimiento
2 cloves garlic, cut in quarters
25 black peppercorns

Select very fresh unopened mushrooms with caps less than 1¼ inches in diameter. Wash, then cut stems, leaving

Boiling Water Bath

Many of the recipes featured in this chapter require a boiling water bath, which helps kill bacteria during the canning process. To do this, place your canner on the stove and fill it a little over halfway with water. Set to boil. Load filled jars, fitted with lids and rings, onto canner rack. Add enough boiling water so water level is at least 1 inch above jar tops. Turn heat to its highest position until water boils vigorously. Then set a timer for the minutes indicated on recipe. Cover canner, and lower heat to maintain a gentle boil throughout processing time. If needed, add more boiling water to keep water level above jars. When jars have been boiled for the recommended time, turn off heat and remove canner lid. Set jars on a towel or cooling rack, leaving at least an inch between each jar.

¼ inch attached to cap. Put mushrooms in a pot on stove-top; add lemon juice and water to cover. Bring to a boil. Simmer 5 minutes, then drain mushrooms. Mix vinegar, olive oil, salt, oregano, and basil in a saucepan. Stir in onions and pimiento, and heat to boiling. Place ¼ garlic clove and 2 to 3 peppercorns in each half-pint jar. Fill jars with mushrooms and hot, well-mixed oil/vinegar solution, leaving a ½-inch headspace. Adjust lids and process in boiling water bath (see opposite page) for 25 minutes.

Makes about 9 half-pints

Cheesy Onion Flatbread

½ cup plus 3 tablespoons honey, divided
2⅓ cups warm water (105° to 115°F), divided
1½ packages active dry yeast
6 tablespoons olive oil, divided
3 cups whole wheat flour
⅓ cup cornmeal
4½ teaspoons coarse salt
3 to 4 cups all-purpose flour, divided
1 large red onion, thinly sliced
1 cup red wine vinegar
Additional cornmeal
1 cup grated Parmesan cheese
½ teaspoon onion salt
Black pepper to taste

1. Place 3 tablespoons honey in large bowl. Pour ⅓ cup water over honey. Do not stir. Sprinkle yeast over water. Let stand about 15 minutes until bubbly. Add remaining

2 cups water, 3 tablespoons olive oil, whole wheat flour, and cornmeal. Mix until well blended. Stir in salt and 2 cups all-purpose flour. Gradually stir in enough remaining flour until mixture clings to side of bowl.

2. Turn dough out onto lightly floured surface. Knead in enough remaining flour to make a smooth and satiny dough, about 10 minutes. Divide dough in half. Place each half in large, lightly greased bowl; turn over to grease surface. Cover; let rise in warm place (80° to 85°F) until doubled.

3. Meanwhile, combine onion, vinegar, and remaining ½ cup honey. Marinate at room temperature at least 1 hour.

4. Grease two 12-inch pizza pans; sprinkle each with additional cornmeal. Stretch dough and pat into pans; create valleys with fingertips. Cover; let rise in warm place until doubled, about 1 hour.

5. Preheat oven to 400°F. Drain onion; scatter over dough. Sprinkle with remaining 3 tablespoons olive oil, cheese, and onion salt. Season with pepper.

6. Bake 25 to 30 minutes or until flatbread is crusty and golden. Cut each flatbread into 8 wedges. Serve warm.

Makes 2 flatbreads, 8 wedges each

Vinegar Vignette

The bloodstream of a healthy adult has a pH that is mildly alkaline—about 7.41. Vinegar is a strongly acidic solution with a pH of around 2.

Cabbage Wedges With Tangy Hot Dressing

1 slice bacon, cut crosswise into ¼-inch strips
2 teaspoons cornstarch
⅔ cup unsweetened apple juice
¼ cup cider or red wine vinegar
1 tablespoon brown sugar
½ teaspoon caraway seeds
1 green onion, thinly sliced
½ head red or green cabbage (about 1 pound), cut into 4 wedges

1. Cook bacon in large skillet over medium heat until crisp. Remove bacon with slotted spoon to paper towel; set aside. Meanwhile, dissolve cornstarch in apple juice in small bowl. Stir in vinegar, brown sugar, and caraway seeds; set aside. Add onion to hot drippings. Cook and stir until onion is soft but not brown.

2. Place cabbage wedges, on flat side, in drippings mixture. Pour cornstarch mixture over cabbage wedges. Cook over medium heat 4 minutes. Carefully turn cabbage wedges over with spatula. Cook 6 minutes more or until cabbage is fork-tender and dressing is thickened.

3. Remove cabbage to cutting board with spatula; carefully cut core away with utility knife. Transfer to warm serving plates. Pour hot dressing over cabbage wedges. Sprinkle with reserved bacon pieces. Garnish as desired. Serve immediately.

Makes 4 side-dish servings

Salads

Marinated Antipasto Pasta Salad

Antipasto Dressing

2 cloves garlic, peeled
⅔ cup white balsamic or white wine vinegar
2 tablespoons Dijon-style mustard
1 teaspoon salt
½ teaspoon sugar
1 cup extra-virgin olive oil

Pasta Salad

4 ounces uncooked mostaccioli or ziti pasta
6 ounces Genoa salami or summer sausage, diced
6 ounces provolone, smoked mozzarella, or regular mozzarella cheese, diced
12 calamata olives
12 red or yellow cherry tomatoes, or a combination
4 bottled pepperoncini peppers, sliced and seeded
Lettuce leaves
Chopped fresh basil

String Bean Salad

Marinate 2 cups cold string beans with French Dressing (see page 157). Add 1 teaspoon finely cut chives. Pile in center of salad dish, and arrange thin slices of radishes overlapping one another around base. Garnish top with radish cut to resemble a tulip.

1. For dressing, drop garlic through feed tube of food processor with the motor running. Process until garlic is minced.

2. Add vinegar, mustard, salt, and sugar; process until combined. With motor running, slowly pour oil through feed tube; process until thickened. Cover; refrigerate 2 hours or up to 1 month.

3. Cook pasta according to package directions; drain and rinse with cool water.

4. Combine pasta, salami, cheese, olives, tomatoes, and pepperoncini in medium bowl. Add dressing; toss well. Cover; refrigerate 2 hours or up to 2 days. Serve on lettuce leaves. Sprinkle with basil.

Makes 6 servings

Roasted Tomato Trick

Roasting store-bought tomatoes is a way to improve their flavor. To do so, cut them in half, brush with olive oil, and sprinkle them with salt to draw out their flavor. Add pepper to taste, and bake at 150°F for 8 to 10 hours. The tomatoes will come out partially dehydrated and shriveled. When cool, cover them with olive oil, and store in refrigerator for up to 2 months.

Spicy Oriental Shrimp Salad

1 head iceberg lettuce
½ cup fresh basil leaves

1/4 cup rice wine vinegar
1 cube fresh ginger (2 inches), peeled
1 tablespoon reduced-sodium soy sauce
3 cloves garlic
2 teaspoons dark sesame oil
1 teaspoon crushed red pepper
28 large shrimp, peeled and deveined
1 to 2 limes, cut into wedges (optional)
Vinaigrette Dressing (recipe follows)

1. Core, rinse, and thoroughly drain lettuce. Refrigerate in airtight container to crisp. Combine basil, vinegar, ginger, soy sauce, garlic, sesame oil, and red pepper in blender or food processor fitted with metal blade. Blend to form rough paste, pulsing blender on and off, scraping sides as needed. Transfer paste to large mixing bowl. Add shrimp and stir until coated. Cover and refrigerate for 2 hours or overnight.

Salt Snippet

A man must eat a peck of salt with his friend, before he knows him.

—Miguel de Cervantes

2. Preheat broiler. Broil shrimp in shallow pan, turning once, just until pink, about 2 minutes each side. Shred lettuce; arrange on 4 plates. Top with cooked shrimp. Garnish with lime, if desired. Serve with Vinaigrette Dressing.

Makes 4 servings

Vinaigrette Dressing

Whisk 3 tablespoons red wine vinegar with 1½ tablespoons olive oil in small bowl until blended.

Jalapeño Coleslaw

6 cups preshredded cabbage or coleslaw mix
2 tomatoes, seeded and chopped
6 green onions, coarsely chopped
*2 jalapeño peppers, finely chopped**
¼ cup cider vinegar
3 tablespoons honey
1 teaspoon salt

*For a milder coleslaw, discard seeds and veins when chopping the jalapeños. Jalapeño peppers can sting and irritate the skin; wear rubber or plastic gloves when handling peppers and do not touch eyes. Wash hands after handling.

1. Combine cabbage, tomatoes, onions, jalapeños, vinegar, honey, and salt in serving bowl; mix well. Cover; refrigerate at least 2 hours.

2. Stir well before serving.

Makes 4 side-dish servings

Marinated Green Beans and Potato Salad

1 pound fresh green beans, washed and trimmed
4 cups red potatoes, cubed and unpeeled
¼ cup red wine vinegar

2 tablespoons olive oil
2 tablespoons fresh lemon juice
4 cloves garlic, crushed
2 teaspoons honey
1 teaspoon salt
1 teaspoon dried dill weed
1 teaspoon dried thyme leaves
½ teaspoon black pepper
4 cups ready-to-use fresh spinach, torn into bite-size pieces
1 medium tomato, cut into wedges

1. Bring 4 quarts water to a boil in Dutch oven. Add green beans; reduce heat to medium and cook, covered, 8 minutes or until beans are crisp-tender. Remove beans with slotted spoon.

2. Add potatoes to same Dutch oven. Cook, covered, 12 to 15 minutes or until potatoes are tender. Drain.

3. Combine vinegar, oil, lemon juice, garlic, honey, salt, dill weed, thyme, and pepper in medium bowl; whisk to combine. Add green beans and potatoes; stir to combine. Cover and refrigerate up to 8 hours, stirring occasionally.

4. To complete recipe, arrange spinach on serving platter. Spoon green bean mixture over spinach. Pour remaining marinade over top. Garnish with tomato wedges.

Makes 6 servings

Dressings

Chicken Salad Dressing

½ cup chicken stock
½ cup vinegar
5 egg yolks, slightly beaten
2 tablespoons mixed mustard
1 teaspoon salt
¼ teaspoon pepper
Few grains of cayenne
½ cup thick cream
⅓ cup melted butter

Combine chicken stock, vinegar, egg yolks, mustard, salt, pepper, and cayenne. Cook over boiling water, stirring constantly until mixture thickens. Strain, add cream and melted butter, then cool.

Vinaigrettes by the Batch

Homemade vinaigrettes are much more pleasant than store-bought dressings. Best of all, you can decide the level of fat (oil) appropriate for your diet. Once you find a favorite homemade vinaigrette, prepare it in large batches and store it in old wine bottles in your refrigerator. It should keep well indefinitely. Bring the vinaigrette to room temperature before serving, or use your microwave on a very low setting to reliquefy the oil in the dressing. Shake well before serving.

Lemon Vinaigrette

½ cup white wine vinegar
1 tablespoon chopped fresh parsley

1 tablespoon olive oil
1 tablespoon honey
1 teaspoon grated lemon peel
1/8 teaspoon black pepper

Whisk vinegar, parsley, oil, honey, lemon peel, and pepper in small bowl until blended.

Makes about 2/3 cup

Grain of Salt Department

If a woman drinks vinegar just before conceiving, she will give birth to a boy.

Basil Vinaigrette Dressing

1/3 cup white wine vinegar
2 tablespoons Dijon mustard
3 cloves garlic, peeled
3/4 cup fresh basil leaves, coarsely chopped
1 cup olive oil
Salt and black pepper to taste

1. Place vinegar, mustard, and garlic in blender or food processor. Cover; blend using on/off pulses until well mixed. Add basil; continue to pulse until mixture is blended.

2. With motor running, slowly pour in olive oil. Season to taste with salt and pepper.

Makes about 1½ cups

Garlic Dressing

3/4 cup olive or vegetable oil
1/4 cup white wine vinegar

1 clove garlic, pressed
1 teaspoon salt
½ teaspoon black pepper

Mix all ingredients in tightly covered jar. (Dressing can be refrigerated up to 2 weeks.)

Makes 1 cup

French Dressing

4 tablespoons olive oil
2 tablespoons vinegar
½ teaspoon salt
¼ teaspoon pepper
Few drops lemon juice (optional)

Put ingredients in small jar and shake. You may want to add a few drops of lemon juice for extra flavor.

Parisian French Dressing

½ cup olive oil
2 tablespoons parsley, finely chopped
5 tablespoons vinegar
½ teaspoon powdered sugar
4 red peppers, finely chopped
1 tablespoon Bermuda onion, finely chopped
8 green peppers, finely chopped
1 teaspoon salt

Mix ingredients in the order given. (The red and green peppers are the small ones found in pepper sauce.) Let stand 1 hour, then stir vigorously for 5 minutes. This dressing is especially good with romaine, chicory, or endive.

Curry Dressing

¾ teaspoon salt
¼ teaspoon pepper
¼ teaspoon curry powder
5 tablespoons olive oil
3 tablespoons vinegar

Mix ingredients in order given, and stir until well blended.

Sauces and Dips

Texas Hot & Tangy BBQ Sauce

¼ cup vegetable oil
2 cups onions, finely chopped
6 cloves garlic, minced
2 cups water
1 can (12 ounces) tomato paste
1 cup packed brown sugar
¾ cup apple cider vinegar
½ cup molasses
¼ cup Worcestershire sauce
2 tablespoons jalapeño pepper sauce
2 teaspoons chili powder
2 teaspoons ground cumin
½ teaspoon ground red pepper

1. Heat oil in large skillet over medium-high heat for 1 minute. Add onions; cook and stir 8 to 10 minutes or until onions begin to brown. Add garlic; cook 2 minutes or until onions are golden. Add remaining ingredients. Stir with wire whisk until well blended. Reduce heat to

medium-low; simmer 15 minutes, stirring occasionally. Cover and remove from heat. Cool 30 minutes.

2. Spoon into 4 labeled 12-ounce containers. Store refrigerated up to 3 weeks.

Makes 5 to 5½ cups

Creamy Cucumber-Yogurt Dip

1 cucumber, peeled, seeded, and finely chopped
Salt
¼ cup chopped fresh chives, divided
1 package (8 ounces) cream cheese, softened
¼ cup plain yogurt
1 tablespoon fresh lemon juice
1½ teaspoons dried mint leaves
Black pepper
Assorted cut-up vegetables

1. Lightly salt cucumber in small bowl; toss. Refrigerate 1 hour. Drain cucumber; dry on paper towels. Set aside.

2. Reserve 1 tablespoon chives for garnish. Place remaining 3 tablespoons chives, cream cheese, yogurt, lemon juice, mint, and pepper in food processor or blender; process until smooth. Stir into cucumber. Cover; refrigerate 1 hour. Spoon dip into glass bowl or gift container; sprinkle

Salt Snippet

Eating too much salt may be contributing to bags under your eyes. Fluid retention in the body, a consequence of too much salt, can result in baggy eyes.

reserved chives over top. Cover and store up to 2 days in refrigerator. Stir before serving with vegetables.

Makes about 2 cups dip

Chili Sauce

12 medium-size ripe tomatoes
1 onion, finely chopped
1 pepper, finely chopped
2 cups vinegar
3 tablespoons sugar
1 tablespoon salt
2 teaspoons ground cloves
2 teaspoons cinnamon
2 teaspoons allspice
2 teaspoons grated nutmeg

Peel and slice tomatoes. Put in a preserving kettle with remaining ingredients. Heat gradually to boiling, and cook slowly for 2½ hours.

Sweet and Sour Sauce

4 teaspoons cornstarch
1 cup water
½ cup sugar
½ cup white vinegar
¼ cup tomato paste

Combine all ingredients in small saucepan. Bring to a boil over high heat, stirring constantly. Boil 1 minute, stirring constantly. Cool.

Makes about 1½ cups (4 servings)

Orange Sauce

2 oranges
1 lemon
2 tablespoons sugar
½ cup chicken broth
3 tablespoons vinegar
1 tablespoon cornstarch

1. Peel off only the colored part of orange and lemon rind, and cut into thin slivers. Put slivers in a saucepan, cover with water, and boil for 5 minutes. Drain, and set aside. Sprinkle sugar on bottom of a heavy pan, heat, and stir until melted and golden brown. Slowly stir in chicken broth and vinegar. Slice and seed peeled oranges and lemons, and add to mixture.

2. Roast the meat of your choice. Pour pan juices into the orange sauce mixture, then add lemon and orange slivers. Bring to a boil. Dissolve cornstarch in 2 tablespoons water, then add to mixture. Stir until thickened, and pour over roasted meat slices.

Condiments

Spicy German Mustard

½ cup mustard seeds
2 tablespoons dry mustard
½ cup cold water
1 cup cider vinegar
1 small onion, chopped (about ¼ cup)
2 cloves garlic, minced

3 tablespoons packed brown sugar
3/4 teaspoon salt
1/4 teaspoon dried tarragon leaves
1/4 teaspoon ground cinnamon

1. Combine mustard seeds, dry mustard, and water in small bowl. Cover; let stand at least 4 hours or overnight.

2. Combine vinegar, onion, garlic, brown sugar, salt, tarragon, and cinnamon in heavy stainless-steel 1-quart saucepan. Bring to a boil over high heat; reduce heat to medium. Boil, uncovered, about 7 to 10 minutes until mixture is reduced by half.

3. Pour vinegar mixture through fine sieve into food processor bowl. Rinse saucepan; set aside. Add mustard mixture to vinegar mixture; process about 1 minute or until mustard seeds are chopped but not puréed. Pour into same saucepan. Cook over low heat until mustard is thick, stirring constantly. Store in airtight container or decorative gift jars up to 1 year in refrigerator.

Makes about 1 cup

Vinegar Vignette

Vinegar played an important role in the early experiments of Louis Pasteur as he developed his germ theory of infection in the mid-1800s.

Mushroom Ketchup

Mushroom ketchup appears as an ingredient in many 18th-century recipes. It can be used as an excellent sauce for cold meats and fowl. Add a dash to sauces and stews for a delectable flavor.

5 pounds mushrooms
2 bay leaves
4 tablespoons salt
1 medium onion, chopped
Rind of 1 lemon, grated
½ cup cider vinegar
½ teaspoon grated horseradish
½ teaspoon ground cloves
½ teaspoon allspice
⅛ teaspoon cayenne

Trim ends of mushroom stems, and wipe them clean (do not peel or wash them). Chop mushrooms, and put them in a bowl with bay leaves and salt. The next day, crush mushrooms (but not bay leaves) with a potato masher. Put in a stainless-steel 1-quart saucepan. Add onion, lemon rind, vinegar, horseradish, cloves, allspice, and cayenne. Bring mixture to a boil, and simmer 30 minutes. Discard bay leaves. Purée in a blender, or leave as is, and pack in hot sterilized jars.

Makes 2 pints

Salt Snippet

In 1931, salt was added to Gerber baby food for the first time, but the idea was resisted by mothers who said it made the food too salty.

Pineapple Chutney

2 pounds fresh pineapple or 1 can crushed pineapple (1 pound 13 ounces)
2⅓ cups brown sugar
1 cup cider vinegar
1 cup dates, diced
1 cup raisins
1 cup sliced almonds
1 tablespoon minced onion
1 teaspoon salt
½ teaspoon ground cloves
½ teaspoon cinnamon
½ teaspoon ground allspice
¼ teaspoon garlic powder
⅛ teaspoon pepper

Mix all ingredients and cook over low heat for 1 hour or until very thick. Stir occasionally to prevent sticking. Seal in preserve glasses, or store in a large crock.

Potato Mayonnaise

1 very small baked potato
1 teaspoon salt
1 teaspoon powdered sugar
1 teaspoon mustard
2 tablespoons vinegar, divided
¾ cup olive oil

Remove skin and mash potato. Add salt, powdered sugar, and mustard. Then add 1 tablespoon vinegar, and press mixture through a fine sieve. Slowly add oil and remaining vinegar.

Pickled Food

Dill Pickles

Use the following quantities for each gallon capacity of your container:

4 pounds pickling cucumbers, 4 inches each
2 tablespoons dill seed or 4 to 5 heads fresh or dry dill weed, divided
2 cloves garlic, divided (optional)
2 dried red peppers, divided (optional)
2 teaspoons whole mixed pickling spices, divided (optional)
½ cup salt
¼ cup vinegar (5 percent)
8 cups water

1. Wash cucumbers. Cut 1/16-inch slice off blossom end and discard. Leave ¼ inch of stem attached. Place half of dill and spices on bottom of a clean container. Add cucumbers and remaining dill and spices. Dissolve salt in vinegar and water, and pour mixture over cucumbers. Add suitable cover and weight. Store where temperature is between 70° and 75°F for about 3 to 4 weeks while fermenting. Temperatures of 55° to 65°F are acceptable, but the fermentation will take 5 to 6 weeks at these temperatures. Avoid temperatures above 80°F, or pickles will

become too soft during fermentation. Fermenting pickles cure slowly. Check container several times a week, and promptly remove surface scum or mold. Caution: If pickles become soft, slimy, or develop a disagreeable odor, discard them.

2. Fully fermented pickles may be stored in their original containers for about 4 to 6 months, provided they are refrigerated and surface scum and molds are removed regularly. Canning fully fermented pickles is a better way to store them. To can them, pour brine into a pan, heat slowly to a boil, and simmer 5 minutes. Filter brine through paper coffee filters to reduce cloudiness, if

Pickling Basics

Just about anything can be pickled using vinegar, but to safely preserve fruits and vegetables, you must use a commercially produced vinegar that has an acetic acid content of 4 to 6 percent, also described as a "40/60 grain strength." Vinegars you make at home are fine for cooking but may be dangerous for preserving because the acetic acid may not be high enough to kill bacteria that can develop while preserved food is stored. Distilled white vinegar is best for pickling because it won't affect the color of the preserved food. Apple cider vinegar will darken most produce. Boiling vinegar will also reduce its acetic acid content; boiled vinegar should not be used for pickling.

desired. Fill jars with pickles and hot brine, leaving a ½-inch headspace. Adjust lids and process in boiling water bath—15 minutes for pints, 20 minutes for quarts (see page 146).

Sweet Gherkin Pickles

7 pounds cucumbers, 1½ inches or less
8 cups sugar, divided
6 cups vinegar (5 percent), divided
¾ teaspoon turmeric
2 cinnamon sticks
½ cup canning or pickling salt
2 teaspoons celery seed
2 teaspoons whole mixed pickling spice
2 teaspoons vanilla (optional)
½ teaspoon fennel (optional)

1. Wash cucumbers. Cut 1/16-inch slice off blossom end and discard, but leave ¼ inch of stem attached. Place cucumbers in large container, and cover with boiling water. Six to 8 hours later and again on the second day, drain and cover with fresh boiling water.

2. On the third day, drain and prick cucumbers with a table fork. Combine 3 cups sugar, 3 cups vinegar, turmeric, and spices. Bring to a boil, then pour mixture over cucumbers. Six to 8 hours later, drain and save the pickling syrup. Add another 2 cups each of sugar and vinegar, and reheat to a boil. Pour over pickles.

3. On the fourth day, drain and save syrup. Add another 2 cups sugar and 1 cup vinegar. Heat to a boil, and pour over pickles. Six to 8 hours later, drain and save pickling syrup. Add 1 cup sugar and vanilla, and heat to a boil. Fill sterile pint jars* with pickles and cover with hot syrup, leaving a ½-inch headspace. Adjust lids and process in boiling water bath for 10 minutes.

Makes 6 to 7 pints

*To sterilize empty jars, put them right side up on the rack in a boiling water canner. Fill canner and jars with hot (not boiling) water to 1 inch above tops of jars. Boil 11 minutes. Remove and drain hot sterilized jars one at a time.

Chinese Mixed Pickled Vegetables

Pickling Liquid

3 cups sugar
3 cups distilled white vinegar
1½ cups water
1½ teaspoons salt

Vegetables

1 large Chinese white radish (about 1 pound), cut into matchstick pieces
3 large carrots, cut into matchstick pieces
1 large cucumber, seeded and cut into matchstick pieces*
4 stalks celery, diagonally cut into ½-inch pieces
8 green onions, diagonally cut into ¼-inch pieces

1 large red pepper, cut into ½-inch pieces
1 large green pepper, cut into ½-inch pieces
4 ounces fresh ginger, peeled and thinly sliced

*Cut cucumber in half lengthwise; remove seeds with spoon.

1. Combine all pickling liquid ingredients in 3-quart saucepan. Bring to a boil over medium heat, stirring occasionally. Cool.

2. Fill 5-quart stockpot or Dutch oven half full with water. Bring to a boil. Add all vegetables. Remove from heat. Let stand 2 minutes.

3. Drain vegetables in large colander. Spread vegetables out onto clean towels; allow to dry 2 to 3 hours.

4. Pack vegetables firmly into clean jars with tight-fitting lids. Pour Pickling Liquid into jars to cover vegetables. Seal jars tightly. Store in refrigerator at least 1 week before using.

Makes 1½ to 2 quarts

Salt Snippet

The phrase "To sit above the salt" means to sit at a dinner table in a place of distinction. Ceremonial tables once featured a salt cellar (a silver center-piece) in the middle of the table. Important guests were seated by custom between this salt cellar and the head of the table, while the less important people sat "below the salt."

Zucchini Chow Chow

2 cups zucchini, thinly sliced
*2 cups yellow summer squash, thinly sliced**
½ cup red onion, thinly sliced
Salt
1½ cups cider vinegar
1 to 1¼ cups sugar
1½ tablespoons pickling spice
1 cup carrots, thinly sliced
1 small red bell pepper, thinly sliced

*If yellow summer squash is not available, increase zucchini to 4 cups.

1. Sprinkle zucchini, summer squash, and onion lightly with salt; let stand in colander 30 minutes. Rinse well with cold water; drain thoroughly. Pat dry with paper towels.

2. Combine vinegar, sugar, and pickling spice in medium saucepan. Bring to a boil over high heat. Add carrots and bell pepper; bring to a boil. Remove from heat; cool to room temperature.

3. Spoon zucchini, summer squash, onion, and carrot mixture into sterilized jars; cover and refrigerate up to 3 weeks.

Makes about 8 cups

Vinegar Vignette

In 1842, New York entrepreneur S. R. Mott introduced Mott's apple cider and Mott's vinegar to the commercial markets.

Piccalilli

6 cups chopped green tomatoes
1½ cups sweet red peppers, chopped
1½ cups green peppers, chopped
2¼ cups onions, chopped
7½ cups cabbage, chopped
½ cup canning or pickling salt
3 tablespoons whole mixed pickling spice
4½ cups vinegar (5 percent)
3 cups brown sugar

Wash, chop, and combine vegetables with salt. Cover with hot water and let stand 12 hours. Drain and press in a clean white cloth to remove all possible liquid. Tie pickling spice loosely in a spice bag, and add bag to combined vinegar and brown sugar. Heat to a boil in a saucepan. Add vegetables, and boil gently over 30 minutes or until the volume of the mixture is reduced by one half. Remove spice bag. Fill hot sterile jars (refer to Sweet Gherkin Pickles on page 168 for how to sterilize jars) with hot mixture, leaving a ½-inch headspace. Adjust lids and process in boiling water bath for 10 minutes (see page 146).

Makes 9 half-pints

Pickled Corn Relish

10 cups fresh-kernel corn (16 to 20 medium-size ears) or 6 packages frozen corn, 10 ounces each
2½ cups sweet red peppers, diced
2½ cups sweet green peppers, diced

2½ cups celery, chopped
1¼ cups onions, diced
1¾ cups sugar
5 cups vinegar (5 percent)
2½ tablespoons canning or pickling salt
2½ teaspoons celery seed
2½ tablespoons dry mustard
1¼ teaspoons turmeric
¼ cup flour (optional)
¼ cup water (optional)

If you're using fresh corn, boil ears for 5 minutes, then dip in cold water. Cut whole kernels from cob, or use packages of frozen corn. Combine peppers, celery, onion, sugar, vinegar, salt, and celery seed in saucepan. Bring to a boil, and simmer 5 minutes, stirring occasionally. Mix mustard and turmeric in ½ cup of simmered mixture. Add this mixture and corn to hot mixture. Simmer another 5 minutes. If desired, thicken mixture with flour paste (¼ cup flour blended with ¼ cup water), and stir frequently. Fill jars with hot mixture, leaving a ½-inch headspace. Adjust lids and process in boiling water bath for 20 minutes (see page 146).

Makes about 9 pints

Candies and Desserts

Vanilla Ice Cream

2½ cups cold whipping cream
1½ cups cold milk
¾ cup sugar

1½ teaspoons vanilla
⅛ teaspoon table salt
Crushed ice
Rock salt

1. Combine whipping cream, milk, sugar, vanilla, and table salt in medium bowl; mix well. Pour mixture into freezer container of ice cream maker. (Do not fill freezer container to top; leave at least 2 inches of headspace above cream mixture to allow room for expansion when mixtures freezes.)

2. Follow manufacturer's directions for assembling ice cream maker. Fill ice cream maker with mixture of 8 parts crushed ice and 1 part rock salt (or follow manufacturer's directions) to a level above the line of the mixture in the freezer container. Pack ice mixture firmly; let stand 5 minutes.

3. Follow manufacturer's directions for freezing ice cream.

4. To harden ice cream, remove dasher; seal freezer container. Drain off ice mixture; repack ice cream maker with 3 parts crushed ice and 1 part rock salt. Let stand for 1 to 2 hours.

Makes 1½ quarts

Grain of Salt Department

If you eat a thimbleful of salt before going to bed, you will make a lover of the one who brings you water in your dreams.

Chocolate Ice Cream: Prepare as directed in step 1, increasing sugar to 1 cup and adding ⅓ cup unsweetened cocoa powder. Proceed as directed above.

Velvet Molasses Candy

3 cups sugar
1 cup water
1 cup molasses
3 tablespoons vinegar
½ teaspoon cream of tartar
½ cup melted butter
¼ teaspoon baking soda
1 teaspoon vanilla
½ teaspoon lemon extract
Few drops of oil of peppermint or wintergreen

Put first 4 ingredients in kettle placed over front of range. As soon as boiling point is reached, add cream of tartar. Boil until a small amount of mixture dropped in cold water becomes brittle. Stir constantly during last part of cooking. When nearly done, add butter and baking soda. Pour into a buttered pan, and pull until porous and light-colored. While pulling, add vanilla, lemon extract, and oil. Cut in small pieces using large shears or a sharp knife, and then arrange on slightly buttered plates to cool.

Butter Taffy

2 cups light brown sugar
¼ cup molasses
2 tablespoons water

2 tablespoons vinegar
7/8 teaspoon salt
1/4 cup butter
2 teaspoons vanilla

Boil first 5 ingredients until a small amount of mixture dropped in cold water becomes brittle. When nearly done, add butter and, just before turning into pan, vanilla. Cool, and mark in squares.

Butterscotch

1 cup sugar
1/2 cup butter
1/4 cup molasses
2 tablespoons water
1 tablespoon vinegar

Boil ingredients together until a small amount of mixture dropped in cold water becomes brittle. Turn into a well-buttered pan. When slightly cool, mark with a sharp-pointed knife in squares. This candy is much improved by cooking a small piece of vanilla bean with other ingredients.

Ice Cream Candy

3 cups sugar
1/2 cup water
1/2 tablespoon vinegar
1/4 teaspoon cream of tartar
Vanilla, orange, or coffee extract; oil of sassafras; or melted chocolate

Boil ingredients together without stirring until a small amount of mixture dropped in cold water becomes brittle. Turn on a well-buttered platter to cool. As edges cool, fold toward center. As soon as it can be handled, pull until white and glossy. While pulling, flavor as desired, using vanilla, orange, or coffee extract; oil of sassafras; or melted chocolate. Cut in sticks or small pieces.

Vinegar Vignette

Rumor has it that Cleopatra dissolved a pearl in a glass of vinegar to prove a point. We're just not sure what the point was.

Popcorn Balls

2 cups sugar
1½ cups water
½ cup white corn syrup
1 tablespoon vanilla
⅓ teaspoon salt
⅓ teaspoon vinegar
5 quarts popped corn

Boil sugar, water, and corn syrup without stirring until thermometer registers 260°F. Add vanilla, salt, and vinegar, and let boil to 264°F. Have corn in a large pan, and gradually pour on the syrup, using a spoon* to turn corn until evenly coated. Make into balls, and let stand in a cold place until brittle.

**Caution*: Do not use your hands as syrup is extremely hot.

Cranberry Apple Nut Pie

Rich Pie Pastry (recipe follows)
1 cup sugar
3 tablespoons all-purpose flour
¼ teaspoon salt
4 cups sliced peeled tart apples (4 large apples)
2 cups fresh cranberries
½ cup golden raisins
½ cup coarsely chopped pecans
1 tablespoon grated lemon peel
2 tablespoons butter
1 egg, beaten

1. Preheat oven to 425°F. Divide pie pastry in half. Roll one half on lightly floured surface to form 13-inch circle. Fit into 9-inch pie plate; trim edges. Reroll scraps and cut into decorative shapes, such as holly leaves and berries, for garnish; set aside.

2. Combine sugar, flour, and salt in large bowl. Stir in apples, cranberries, raisins, pecans, and lemon peel; toss well. Spoon fruit mixture into unbaked pie crust. Dot with butter. Roll remaining half of pie pastry on lightly floured surface to form 11-inch circle. Place over filling. Trim and seal edges; flute. Cut 3 slits in center of top crust. Moisten pastry cutouts and use to decorate top crust as desired. Lightly brush top crust with egg.

3. Bake 35 to 40 minutes or until apples are tender when pierced with fork and pastry is golden brown. Cool in pan on wire rack. Serve warm or cool completely.

Makes 1 (9-inch) pie

Rich Pie Pastry

2 cups all-purpose flour
1/4 teaspoon salt
6 tablespoons cold butter
6 tablespoons shortening or lard
6 to 8 tablespoons cold water

Combine flour and salt in medium bowl. Cut in butter and lard with pastry blender or 2 knives until mixture resembles coarse crumbs. Sprinkle water, 1 tablespoon at a time, over flour mixture, mixing until flour is moistened. Shape dough into a ball. Roll, fill, and bake as recipe directs.

Makes pastry for 1 (9-inch) double pie crust

Note: For single crust, cut recipe in half.

Salt Snippet

In 1694, Parliament doubled the salt tax, which was in place throughout England, in order to help fund the ongoing war with France.

More Salt and Vinegar Recipes

Encore Eggs Benedict

Hollandaise Sauce (recipe follows)
8 eggs
16 slices Canadian bacon
4 English muffins, split, toasted, and buttered

1. Prepare Hollandaise Sauce.

2. Bring 2 to 3 inches water to a boil in medium saucepan over medium-high heat. Reduce heat to a simmer. Break 1 egg into small dish. Holding dish close to surface of simmering water, carefully slip egg into water. Repeat with second egg. Cook 3 to 5 minutes or until yolks are just set. Remove eggs and drain on paper towels. Repeat with remaining eggs.

3. Meanwhile, cook bacon in large skillet over medium-low heat, turning occasionally.

4. Top each English muffin half with 2 slices bacon, 1 poached egg, and 1 tablespoon Hollandaise Sauce. Serve immediately.

Makes 4 servings

Hollandaise Sauce

3 egg yolks
1 tablespoon lemon juice
1 teaspoon dry mustard
¼ teaspoon salt
Dash ground red pepper (optional)
½ cup (1 stick) butter, cut into eighths

1. Beat together egg yolks, lemon juice, mustard, salt, and pepper in small saucepan until blended. Add ¼ cup butter.

2. Cook over low heat, stirring with wire whisk until butter is melted. Slowly add remaining ¼ cup butter; whisk constantly until butter is melted and sauce is thickened.

Makes ¾ cup

Variation: Substitute smoked salmon for Canadian bacon. Use approximately 2 ounces smoked salmon per serving.

Moussaka

1 large eggplant
2½ teaspoons salt, divided
2 large zucchini
2 large russet potatoes, peeled
½ cup olive oil, divided
1½ pounds ground beef or lamb
1 large onion, chopped
2 cloves garlic, minced
1 cup chopped tomatoes
½ cup dry red or white wine
¼ cup chopped fresh parsley
¼ teaspoon ground cinnamon
⅛ teaspoon black pepper
1 cup grated Parmesan cheese, divided
4 tablespoons butter or margarine, divided
⅓ cup all-purpose flour
¼ teaspoon ground nutmeg
2 cups milk

1. Cut eggplant lengthwise into ½-inch-thick slices. Place in large colander; sprinkle with 1 teaspoon salt. Drain 30 minutes. Cut zucchini lengthwise into ⅜-inch-thick slices. Cut potatoes lengthwise into ¼-inch-thick slices.

2. Heat ¼ cup oil in large skillet over medium heat until hot. Add potatoes in single layer. Cook 5 minutes

per side or until tender and lightly browned. Remove potatoes from skillet; drain on paper towels. Add more oil to skillet, if needed. Cook zucchini 2 minutes per side or until tender. Drain on paper towels. Add more oil to skillet. Cook eggplant 5 minutes per side or until tender. Drain on paper towels. Drain oil from skillet; discard.

3. Heat skillet over medium-high heat just until hot. Add beef, onion, and garlic; cook and stir 5 minutes or until meat is no longer pink. Pour off drippings. Stir in tomatoes, wine, parsley, 1 teaspoon salt, cinnamon, and pepper. Bring to a boil over high heat. Reduce heat to low. Simmer 10 minutes or until liquid is evaporated.

4. Preheat oven to 325°F. Grease 13×9-inch baking dish. Arrange potatoes in bottom; sprinkle with ¼ cup cheese. Top with zucchini and ¼ cup cheese, then eggplant and ¼ cup cheese. Spoon meat mixture over top.

5. To prepare sauce, melt butter in medium saucepan over low heat. Blend in flour, remaining ½ teaspoon salt and nutmeg with wire whisk. Cook 1 minute, whisking constantly. Gradually whisk in milk. Cook over medium heat until mixture boils and thickens, whisking constantly. Pour sauce evenly over meat mixture in dish; sprinkle with remaining ¼ cup cheese. Bake 30 to 40 minutes or until hot and bubbly. Garnish as desired.

Makes 6 to 8 servings

Soft Pretzels

1 package (16 ounces) hot roll mix plus ingredients to prepare mix
1 egg white
2 teaspoons water
2 tablespoons each assorted coatings: coarse salt, grated Parmesan cheese, sesame seeds, poppy seeds, dried oregano leaves

1. Prepare hot roll mix according to package directions.

2. Preheat oven to 375°F. Spray baking sheets with nonstick cooking spray; set aside.

3. Divide dough equally into 16 pieces; roll each piece with hands to form a rope, 7 to 10 inches long. Place on prepared cookie sheets; form into desired shape (hearts, rings, pretzels, etc.).

4. Beat together egg white and water in small bowl until foamy. Brush onto dough shapes; sprinkle each shape with 1½ teaspoons of one of the coatings.

Roasted Pumpkin Seeds

Take out seeds from a pumpkin, then remove pulp from seeds. Rinse seeds, and spread them on a paper towel to dry. When dry, spread them in a thin layer on a cookie sheet. Sprinkle generously with salt, then bake at 300°F. Turn seeds once or twice with a spatula while baking. Remove from oven when seeds are crisp and just golden brown.

5. Bake until golden brown, about 15 minutes. Serve warm or at room temperature.

Makes 8 servings

Raspberry Shrub

Farming can be hot, dry work, and this drink was reportedly a favorite among farmers during haying season. The drink has a sweet-and-sour tang.

1 quart raspberries
3 cups sugar
1 cup vinegar
1 cup water

Mix all ingredients together, and let stand until sugar melts and berries release their juices. Heat mixture to just boiling, then remove from heat, and strain. Let cool, then serve over ice. Dilute mixture with plain water, seltzer water, juice, or ginger ale.

Makes 2 quarts

Salt Snippet

A healthy human body has about 4 ounces of salt floating around in it. A lack of salt in the body, which can be caused by disease or diet, may affect muscle contraction, blood circulation, digestion, and heart rhythm.

Index